PRAISE FOR *CRUCIAL ACCOUNTABILITY*

"The revolutionary ideas in this book demonstrate how these moments of potential breakdown are, in fact, opportunities for breakthrough. The wisdom this book offers will not only save countless imperiled relationships, it will strengthen the world by profoundly strengthening its fundamental building blocks—our families, neighborhoods, communities, and workplaces."

—Stephen R. Covey, author of
The 7 Habits of Highly Effective People

"The tools and concepts of *Crucial Accountability* have proven to be extraordinarily effective in preparing our leaders to manage change and improve results. We expect this new book to take us to the next level in driving accountability."

—Mike Redenbaugh, CEO, Bell Helicopter

"The greatest test of a relationship is what happens when someone lets you down. Yet these are the moments of greatest opportunity. By learning to manage accountability, you can unleash the true potential of a relationship or organization and move it to the next level. Never again will you have to choose between candor and kindness. This book teaches you that you can win by using both."

—Ken Blanchard, coauthor of
The One Minute Manager® and
The Secret: What Great Leaders Know—and Do

"I've got no patience for foo-foo. This book is the real deal—it has immediate practicality. This is not fluff. The authors spent over 10,000 hours observing individuals who had been

identified as the best at engaging in difficult but necessary 1st option: Accountability discussions where everyone wins and relationships are ultimately strengthened. Read it, underline it, learn from it. It's a gem."

—Mike Murray, VP Human Resources and
Administration, Microsoft (retired)

"Hot-headed players. Bad refs. Energetic coaches. Anxious team owners. Watch out! This book redefines how we all relate to each other. Read it now or get lost in the dust."

—Danny Ainge, Executive Director,
Basketball Operations Boston Celtics

"Brutal honesty is easy. Suffering in silence takes no skill. Achieving absolute honesty while maintaining complete respect requires skill. And useful skills is what this book offers. It redefines how we relate to each other at work and at home. When *Crucial Accountability* becomes required reading for everyone, the result will be overwhelming increases in productivity and prosperity."

—Harry Paul, coauthor, *FISH! A Remarkable
Way to Boost Morale and Improve Results*

"I've seen firsthand how these ideas can change a company for the better. But *Crucial Accountability* is not for the faint-hearted leader. It starts with the CEO, demands greater openness of all leaders, and removes people's chronic excuses for failed results in the past. It also creates a new climate of willingness on everyone's part to confront tough issues with colleagues. It works. It profoundly affects performance. I highly recommend it."

—Russell K. Tolman, President & CEO Cook Children's
Health Care System, Fort Worth, Texas

"This book bristles with ideas and insights. The authors build a compelling set of skills based on solid research and a deep understanding of psychological functioning. Think of the most talented leaders, parents, or spouses you know—these are the skills they use. It is a 'must-read' book for anyone who has to make decisions about people and to be socially effective."

—Dr. Philip Zimbardo, author, host of the PBS series
Discovering Psychology, past President of the
American Psychological Association,
Professor of Psychology, Stanford University

"The compelling organizational, often life-saving, skills presented in this book are the most important contribution to improving human interactions in healthcare I have seen in my career. I am confident that if all healthcare providers adopt these strategies there will be a dramatic improvement in patient safety and satisfaction—the 'bottom line' in healthcare that really counts."

—Wanda Johanson, President,
American Association of Critical-Care Nurses

"To sustain a learning culture, the tools of *Crucial Conversations* and now *Crucial Accountability* are a must-have! Read on and find out how *Crucial Accountability* can add to your team's effectiveness!"

—Charlotte Roberts, coauthor of
The Fifth Discipline Field Book

"Clear and consistent communication can work magic in an organization . . . but only if leaders have the courage and skills to set clear expectations and hold all individuals accountable. *Crucial Accountability* gives leaders simple, effective tools to address tough problems and move to resolution."

—Quint Studer, CEO, Studer Group
and author of *Hardwiring Excellence*

"There is no way to overestimate the power of language and conversation to transform our lives. *Crucial Accountability* offers a proven and powerful way to have more authentic relationships in a way that brings more care and compassion into the world."

—Peter Block, author of *Flawless Consulting,*
Stewardship and *The Answer to How Is Yes*

"*Crucial Accountability* lays out not only the need for holding others to their word but also practical steps on how to do so. People who say they believe in accountability and execution, but struggle with how to do it, should have this book on their desk. It goes beyond conceptual 'solutions' and provides simple techniques and approaches that anyone can use."

—Paul McKinnon,
Head of Human Resources, Citigroup, Inc.

"They've done it again! With *Crucial Accountability*, the authors have once again delivered practical and proven tools to immediately improve individual performance and organization success. This will be the most recommended and most effective resource in my library."

—Stacey Allerton Firth, Vice President,
Human Resources, Ford of Canada

Crucial
Accountability

Also by the Authors

Crucial Conversations:
Tools for Talking When Stakes Are High

Influencer:
The New Science of Leading Change

Change Anything:
The New Science of Personal Success

Crucial Accountability

Tools for Resolving Violated Expectations, Broken Commitments, and Bad Behavior

SECOND EDITION

Kerry Patterson, Joseph Grenny,
David Maxfield, Ron McMillan,
and Al Switzler

First edition published as
Crucial Confrontations

New York Chicago San Francisco Lisbon London Madrid Mexico City
Milan New Delhi San Juan Seoul Singapore Sydney Toronto

9 10 11 12 13 14 15 DOC 20 19 18 17 16

ISBN 978-0-07-182931-1 (paperback)
MHID 0-07-182931-8 (paperback)

ISBN 978-0-07-183060-7 (hardcover)
MHID 0-07-183060-X (hardcover)

e-ISBN 978-0-07-183059-1
e-MHID 0-07-183059-6

Library of Congress Cataloging-in-Publication Data

Patterson, Kerry, 1946-
 [Crucial confrontations]
 Crucial accountability: tools for resolving violated expectations, broken commitments, and bad behavior/by Kerry Patterson, Joseph Grenny, Ron McMillan, Al Switzler, and, David Maxfield. — 2e [edition].
   pages cm
 Includes bibliographical references and index.
 ISBN-13: 978-0-07-183060-7 (alk. paper)
 ISBN-10: 0-07-183060-X (alk. paper)
 ISBN-13: 978-0-07-182931-1 (pbk. : alk. paper)
 ISBN-10: 0-07-182931-8 (pbk. : alk. paper) 1. Interpersonal confrontation.
2. Interpersonal communication. 3. Interpersonal relations. 4. Communication in management. 5. Communication in organizations. I. Title.
 HM1121.C78 2013
 302—dc23

                                                                2013006224

McGraw-Hill Education books are available at special quantity discounts to use as premiums and sales promotions or for use in corporate training programs. To contact a representative, please e-mail us at bulksales@mcgraw-hill.com.

This book is printed on acid-free paper.

First edition published as *Crucial Confrontations*

We dedicate this book to

THE WORLD'S BEST LEADERS
Those managers, supervisors, associates,
team members, parents, colleagues, and
technicians who have routinely
stepped up to tough (even hostile)
problems and skillfully held
others accountable.

Thank you for your examples.
Thank you for helping us learn.

Contents

Foreword   xiii
Preface   xvii
Acknowledgments   xviii

Introduction: What Is Crucial Accountability?
And Who Cares?   1

Part One: Work on Me First
What to Do Before an Accountability Discussion   15

Chapter 1: Choose *What* and *If*
How to Know What *Conversation to Hold
and* If *You Should Hold It*   17

Chapter 2: Master My Stories
*How to Get Your Head Right Before
Opening Your Mouth*   47

Part Two: Create Safety
What to Do During an Accountability Discussion   73

Chapter 3: Describe the Gap
How to Start an Accountability Discussion   75

Chapter 4: Make It Motivating
How to Help Others Want to Take Action   105

Chapter 5: Make It Easy
How to Make Keeping Commitments (Almost) Painless   137

Chapter 6: Stay Focused and Flexible

What to Do When Others Get Sidetracked,
Scream, or Sulk 165

Part Three: Move to Action

What to Do After an Accountability Discussion 193

Chapter 7: Agree on a Plan and Follow Up

How to Gain Commitment and Move to Action 195

Chapter 8: Put It All Together

How to Solve Big, Sticky, Complicated Problems 211

Chapter 9: The 12 "Yeah-Buts"

How to Deal with the Truly Tough 225

Appendix A: Where Do You Stand?

A Self-Assessment for Measuring Your Skills for Holding an
Accountability Discussion Skills 247

Appendix B: Six-Source Diagnostic Questions

The Six-Source Model 252

Appendix C: When Things Go Right 256

Appendix D:

Discussion Questions for Reading Groups 263

Notes 265

Index 267

Foreword

As I read this book, my mind kept reverting to a particular image. Namely, J. D. Watson and Francis Crick as they relentlessly pursued the mystery of life . . . and finally struck upon the double-helix structure of DNA. The world has never been the same. Next stop . . . Stockholm in December.

I don't know whether the authors of this book will get the call that confirms a Nobel, but there's a part of me that thinks it's their just deserts for this magnificent and groundbreaking masterwork.

An absurd claim?

I think not.

War and peace, wellness and extreme physical and mental malaise, marriage and divorce, abject failure and Olympian success . . . all these profound subjects at their core depend upon functioning—or malfunctioning—human relationships. Dyads: a couple. Little organizations: a 20-table restaurant or 20-person finance department. Giant organizations . . . an army or a Fortune 50 corporation. Nations on the brink of war and genocide.

Enter our new Watson and Crick and the essential element of the organizational DNA: the DNA of effective accountability discussions.

Some renowned management experts have made careers out of their belief, "Get the strategy right . . . and the rest will take care of itself." Others have said, "Strategy, smattergy . . . it's the core business processes that explain the divergence between winners and losers." And then there are those that claim that leader selection has no peer in explaining various degrees of organizational effectiveness.

Doubtless there is truth in all the above. (I've held various of these positions over the years . . . each passionately.) But then again, perhaps all such "magisterial" concepts aimed at explaining differences in organizational outcomes miss the boat. Perhaps the idea of organizational DNA that makes for stellar outcomes is Absent Without Leave.

Until now.

Yes, I'm that bullish on *Crucial Accountability*. (Perhaps because I've seen so many of my own brilliant strategies evaporate in the space of minutes—seconds—as I screwed up an accountability discussion with a peer or key employee. Again . . . and again.)

So why did we have to wait until this moment for this book? Perhaps it's the times. We used to live in a more tolerant world. Buildups to war could last decades. Smoldering corporate ineffectiveness could take eons to burst into flame. Lousy marriages festered for years and then more years.

No more. The marketplace is unforgiving. One strike—whether new-product foul-up or terrorist with dirty bomb—and you're (we're!) out. Thus continual organizational effectiveness—which is, after all, nothing more than human-relations effectiveness—is of the utmost urgency, from CIA headquarters to Walmart headquarters.

Crucial Accountability is an original and a bold leap forward. No doubt at all. But like all good science, it is built on a rock-solid base of what has come before. The neat trick here is imaginatively applying the best of psychological and social-psychological research over the last half century to this very particular, precisely defined topic . . . crucial accountability—on topics such as performance and trust—that promote or destroy relational or organizational effectiveness.

The basic hypothesis is profound. The application of proven research is masterful. The explanations and supporting stories are compelling and lucid. The translation of the research and stories into practical ideas and sound advice that can be implemented by those of us who have floundered on these paths for decades is nothing short of breathtaking.

Hey, if you read only one "management" book . . . this decade . . . I'd insist that it be *Crucial Accountability*.

Tom Peters
Lenox, MA

Preface:
A Note to Our Readers

This book is a companion to *Crucial Conversations: Tools for Talking When Stakes Are High*. Those who have read this offering or heard about it or bought the action figures are sure to wonder, "What's the difference between crucial conversations and crucial accountability?" We're glad you asked.

Crucial conversations deal with high-stakes interactions where emotions run strong and opinions vary. Crucial accountability deals with a subset of these interactions. After parties have come to a common understanding and assignments have been made—meaning things are on course—someone fails to complete his or her assignment.

All accountability discussions start with the question "Why didn't you keep your commitment?" And they end, not merely when a solution is reached, but when it's done in such a manner that both parties are able to comply and the relationship is strengthened. In short, accountability discussions are the prickly, complicated, and often frightening performance discussions that keep us up nights.

Now, here's how the two books relate. This book draws on the principles found in *Crucial Conversations*—with an occasional and brief review of those pivotal concepts. With that said, almost all of the material you'll find here deals with the challenges associated with violated commitments and, as such, is new and stand-alone. Pick up this book, read it, put the ideas into action, and you'll never walk away from another broken promise again.

Acknowledgments

Here are just a few of our 100+ colleagues on the VitalSmarts team who are as committed to this work as any of the authors:

James Allred, Terry Brown, Mike Carter, Lance Garvin, Jeff Gibbs, Justin Hale, Emily Hoffman, Jeff Johnson, Todd King, Brittney Maxfield, Mary McChesney, John Minert, David Nelson, Stacy Nelson, Rich Rusick, Andy Shimberg, Mindy Waite, Yan Wang, Steve Willis, Mike Wilson, Paul Yoachum, and Rob Youngberg.

Thanks also to our U.S. associates who are gifted teachers and powerful influencers:

Doug Finton

Ilayne Geller

Tamara Kerr

Richard Lee

Simon Lia

Murray Low

Jim Mahan

Margie Mauldin

Paul McMurray

Jim Munoa

Larry Peters

Shirley Poertner

Mike Quinlan

Kurt Southam

Neil Staker

And finally we express gratitude to the partners and friends who have supported our work around the globe:

Australia—Geoff Flemming and Grant Donovan

Brazil—Josmar Arrais

China—Jenny Xu
Egypt—Hisham El Bakry
France—Cathia Birac and Dagmar Doring
India—Yogesh Sood
Indonesia—Nugroho Supangat
Italy—Giovanni Verrecchia
Malaysia—V. Sitham
Netherlands—Sander van Eijnsbergen and Willeke Kremer
Poland—Marek Choim
Singapore—James Chan
South Africa—Helene Vermaak and Jay Owens
South Korea—Ken Gimm
Switzerland—Arturo Nicora
Thailand—TP Lim
U.K.—Grahame Robb and Richard Pound

Introduction

What Is Crucial Accountability?

And Who Cares?

STEPPING UP TO VIOLATED EXPECTATIONS

Sooner or later it happens to all of us. You're politely standing in line and a fellow cuts in front of you. What the . . . ? Well, you'll just have to say something.

"Just where do you think you're going?" you bark. *"The line ends here. It begins there!"*

To punctuate your point you aggressively shake your finger in the direction of the beginning of the line. Nobody is going to play you for a fool.

It turns out you're not alone in your impressive display of courage. Years ago we asked people at a local mall if they would speak up to a line cutter. Almost all of them said they would. Nobody wants to be a patsy. But then, later on, when we had people actually cut in front of people standing in line at a movie theater, *not one person spoke up*. Not one.

Of course, not all the people we studied remained totally silent. Several made faces or turned to a friend next to them and griped about the intrusion. They reserved the right to bad-mouth line cutters behind their backs.

And then came a breakthrough. After changing the age, gender, and size of the line cutters in trial after trial—to no effect—a woman finally spoke up. She tapped the shoulder of the woman who cut in front of her and asked, "Who does your hair?" (Check out a re-creation of this experiment in the video "Whose Line Is It Now?" at http://www.vitalsmarts.com/bookresources.)

IT'S A MATH THING

Later, when members of our research team asked people why they had gone to silence in the face of someone violating a social norm—not to mention violating the sacred line rights of the subject in question—most commented that the mental math they performed at the time of the infraction suggested it wasn't worth the effort. It was only a minor infraction of little consequence, and speaking up might actually cause a problem. Ergo, go to silence.

So we upped the ante. We left the mall and sat down next to students at a university library and made loud noises. Once again, nobody said anything. Members of our research team practically held a party in a location that most of us see as the very temple of silence, and yet nobody said a word. It was a library, and we were talking REALLY LOUD! Still nothing.

So we snuggled up close to library patrons seated at the tables around us and read from their books—occasionally underlining a passage or two. Again, little direct dialogue. Next we went to the student union building, sat next to people seated in the cafeteria, asked them about the food they were eating, and then, you guessed it, started sampling French fries and pie from their tray. Still, few spoke up.

As clinically passive as these research subjects seem, their silence was unique neither to the population we studied nor to any particular decade. As it turns out, 30 years after we started this line of research, you can watch a number of TV programs that are devoted to this very phenomenon. The producers hide their cameras, pay actors to do something strange, antisocial, or politically incorrect in front of innocent observers, and then record the antics that follow.

When faced with scenarios even more bizarre than eating from a stranger's plate (e.g., observing a possible abduction, seeing someone collapse on the sidewalk, listening to someone make a horribly racist comment, etc.), the majority of today's onlookers remain silent. You have to put someone's life in danger before innocent observers will utter a word—and even then, most people don't say anything.

But what if the scenario you're watching is not taken from a mall study or TV program and the stakes are both genuine and high—people could die if someone doesn't speak up. How would you feel about research subjects who remain silent under these conditions? Better yet, would you yourself keep quiet even when doing so could cause others harm?

To answer the first question, you don't have to go very far. Simply visit a patient in a nearby hospital. Attached to the door-frame of nearly every hospital room in the Western world you'll find a hand pump filled with sanitizing solution. Each healthcare professional entering the room, by hospital policy, is supposed to sanitize his or her hands to help avert passing infections from one patient to the next.

The good doctor entering the room you're observing has just examined three patients down the hallway who are suffering, in turn, from cholera, meningitis, and yellow fever. He is now coming in to examine (read *touch*) your father-in-law. Watch as the physician enters the room and fails to wash his hands. He walks right past the bottle of sanitizing solution and toward your father-in-law. Fortunately, it's your lucky day. An attending nurse observes this violation of protocol. Surely she'll speak up.

Or will she?

Most won't. Once again, it's a math thing. It's a physician whom the nurse has to hold accountable, and the physician could become annoyed, even offended, at the mere hint of a misstep. Heaven only knows that incurring the wrath of a physician can wreck a career. Plus there's always a chance that the diseases won't be passed on so easily. And then again, maybe the doctor did wash his hands somewhere out of sight. And so unfold the mental calculations of the nurse who opts to join the ranks of the silent.

THE SILENT MAJORITY

Now, lest you think we're being unfair to healthcare, let's make it clear that the habit of not holding others accountable in the face of a possible disaster is not unique to hand hygiene nor, for that matter, theater protocols. For over three decades following that first day in the mall, we've routinely conducted studies examining people's willingness to step up to the plate and hold others accountable. It turns out it's remarkably easy to find conditions where people don't speak up to individuals who are violating a promise, breaking a commitment, behaving badly, or otherwise not living up to expectations.

For instance, two-thirds of those we polled suggested that they can hardly stand going to family holiday gatherings because one or more of their relatives will do something offensive, yet nobody dares say anything. Someone tried to say something once, but it led to a nasty argument, and so now people clam up, suffer the intolerable tension, and leave the gathering as soon as possible.[1]

In a similar vein, the vast majority of employees we polled no longer talk politics at work because coworkers often become too forceful, even obnoxious, when expressing their views. Rather than deal with coworkers who use abrasive debate tactics, they simply avoid political discussions altogether.[2]

Speaking of workplace reticence, 93 percent of the people we polled work day in and day out with a person they find hard to work with, but nobody holds the person accountable because other employees believe that it's too dangerous.[3] And speaking of danger, when it comes to risky acts, every day tens of thousands of people watch their coworkers perform unsafe work practices, yet they remain silent. After all, you don't rat out a coworker, and, well, you certainly don't talk directly to a peer about violating a rule. It's simply not done. You don't want to look sanctimonious.

Or how about this problem? Over 70 percent of the project managers we studied admitted that they were going to be hopelessly late on their current project because the deadline they were facing was insane but nobody spoke up when it was first created. Nobody said to the bosses, "Could you please involve us before you pick delivery dates?" In addition, when cross-functional team members put the project at risk by failing to meet their commitments, we found there was less than a 20 percent chance anyone would approach them honestly and discuss the broken commitment.[4]

The headlines reveal that this epidemic of silence cuts across virtually every aspect of our lives. For instance, on the morning of January 13, 1982, a jumbo jet crashed into a bridge connecting Virginia to Washington. All but 5 of the 79 people on board died. Later, investigators learned that the copilot was concerned about the ice building up on the wings, mentioned it, was ignored, and then didn't bring it up again for fear of being too forceful with a pilot. Seventy-four people died from a single case of silence.[5]

Or how about the granddaddy of all flight debacles? The space shuttle *Challenger* broke into pieces in front of a horrified nation because, as we later learned, several engineers were concerned that the O-rings might malfunction but they didn't say anything because nobody pushed back honestly with the bosses.[6]

And why? Because with certain people and circumstances you just don't bring up infractions. Not with a boss. Not with a pilot. Not with a doctor. Not with a colleague or relative. Oh yes, and not with someone cutting in line.

DEALING WITH DISAPPOINTMENTS

So what would it take to change the mental math that is so frequently working against us? Is it possible to turn the cost-benefit analysis around and return accountability to a woefully silent world?

To answer this, let's return to our first study—the one where subjects believed that speaking up to a line cutter wasn't worth the risk. What if we taught people standing in line a script for dealing with a line cutter? If we showed them a successful interaction, would they change their math enough to now stand up to someone who cuts in front of them?

To find out, we added a twist to our research design. For our second round of line cutting, we cut in front of a research colleague who was queuing up at the movie theater just like everyone else. Rather than remain silent (as was the established norm), our colleague was instructed to abruptly say, "Hey buddy, get to the end of the line like everyone else!" The offender (also from our research team) then apologized and scurried to the end of the line.

And now for the fun part. We waited a few minutes and then cut in front of the person standing directly behind our rather forceful colleague. Would the subject we cut in front of now speak up, maybe even using the same script he or she had observed? The script had worked. The line cutter had gone to the end of the line without causing a fuss. The mental math had to be somewhat different.

But apparently not enough different. Nobody who observed the abrupt model said a word when confronted by a line cutter. Subjects explained that they didn't want to act like the jerk whom they had observed bluntly dealing with the line cutter. That was part of the reason most people remained silent in the first place. They had no desire to behave like a thug, nor did they want to risk the ugly confrontation that might follow a blunt verbal attack. They already knew how to be abrasive. Teaching them another abrasive script changed neither their mental math nor their behavior.

In fact, most people who routinely revert to silence do so as a result of similar calculations. They have been let down, left holding the bag, or otherwise treated poorly until they eventually tire of others disappointing them. Then, one day the problem reemerges, and they blow a gasket. They trade silence for their favorite form of verbal violence by raising their voice at their relative, or barking at a coworker, or perhaps acting far too smug with their boss. And then bad things happen.

Maybe you've experienced the same phenomenon. Someone repeatedly violates an expectation, and you play nice for several weeks until one day you can take it no longer, and so you launch a verbal attack on the offending party. The tongue-lashing seems to be going well until you notice that everyone in the surrounding area is staring at you, not the guy who kept breaking commitments. You've become the bad person in this scene. How did that ever happen?

Learning from your mistake, your mental math changes to a predictable and unpromising formula. You conclude that it's better to remain mum than look the fool. It'll be a cold day in you know where before you speak up again.

Here's the takeaway. Most of us have been disappointed or treated poorly by others and have experienced both ineffective options—(1) perpetuating the problem by saying nothing and (2) speaking up and creating a new problem. As a result, we feel trapped between two bad alternatives. We would like to say something—but not something abrasive or rude that could lead to an altercation.

With this in mind, we started our third research trial with a new technique. This time we modeled an effective option to the people in the queue. We cut in front of a colleague who had been instructed to give a direct, but civil, response to the line cutter. He was to politely state: "I'm sorry; perhaps you're unaware. We've been standing in line for over 30 minutes." (Note the civil tone and assumption of innocence.) The line cutter then apologized and scurried to the end of the line.

Once again, we let a few minutes pass before we cut in front of a person who had observed the staged interaction and waited to see how our research subjects would react. Given the better choice of words and delivery, would the research subjects' mental math change to the point where they finally spoke up? Or would they still remain silent? After all, silence still costs nothing more than a few additional moments in line.

Not only did more than 80 percent of the research subjects who observed the polite interaction break from tradition and say something to the line cutter, but they used the exact same words they had heard: "I'm sorry, perhaps you're unaware . . ."

It was amazing! Provide individuals who have been disappointed or poorly treated with something to say and a way to say it that leads to the result they want, and their mental math changes. Better yet, their behavior changes. People now believe it's in their best interest to step up to violated promises, broken commitments, and bad behavior. And they do.

CRUCIAL ACCOUNTABILITY

It took us a while, but we had finally uncovered a method for getting people to step up to a problem and hold the other person accountable. However, let's not get too excited. After all, our research had been done with a rather trivial problem where merely pointing out the infraction in a civil manner appeared to work, and so people gave it a try. When it came to holding others accountable, we had only learned to walk.

But what if the crucial conversation involved a more serious and complicated infraction? Could you get people to hold others accountable for their actions when a single civil sentence might not be enough to solve the problem? Could we advance from walking to running?

We were soon to find out. Fresh off our line-cutting success, we received a phone call from a midwestern plant manager who worked in a large manufacturing organization that, according to him, had lost any semblance of accountability.

"You'd have to kill a person to get fired around here," the plant manager said.

"A really popular person," the HR director added with a smirk.

This was going to be a challenge. We were confident that people can learn accountability skills (under the proper circumstances), but what if you point out a broken commitment and the other person isn't motivated to do the correct thing, or she doesn't know what to do, or she brings up another issue, or she gets upset that you're even talking about the problem in the first place? How do you hold others accountable when the conversation becomes fluid and complicated?

POSITIVE DEVIANCE

To learn the best practices involved in lengthier, more complex accountability discussions, we asked the plant manager if there were any supervisors in the building who actually did hold others accountable in a way that worked, and if so, would he allow us to watch them in action?

At first, he pointed out that his supervisors fell into two camps. You had those whom he described as running a "country club." These were individuals who were so pleasant that they created good morale, but they only achieved mediocre results because they rarely held others accountable. In the second camp you'd find leaders who could solve problems all right, but only by demeaning and threatening others in a way that led to low morale and eventually to poor results.

But then the plant manager thought of a few individuals who routinely found a way to hold others accountable, and they did so in a manner that not only solved the problem but also improved their relationship. They found a way to be both honest and respectful—and rarely had to invoke their formal authority to get things done.

And thus began our first attempt to study "positive deviants"—people who struggle in the same circumstances as others but find a way to produce remarkably better results. In a world filled with failure, we learned to find a handful of individuals who succeed in the face of danger, observe them in action, identify exactly what they do that differentiates them from their less successful peers, and then teach these unique actions to others. In short, we came up with a plan to study the best, share the wealth, and eventually infect an entire organization with healthy behavior.

It was worth a shot. If we could identify accountability skills that actually worked and taught them to others, we predicted that people would watch the skills in action and eventually change their mental math. In time, with new and positive expectations, they would step up to accountability discussions as a matter of course.

For months we compared the actions of positive deviants with everyone else's actions. Eventually we succeeded. One by one, action by action, we began to identify skills that positive deviants routinely employed as they stepped up to others and held others accountable—skills that others failed to use.

For instance, suppose that one of the individuals you're observing in action points out an infraction to a coworker and the offending party doesn't appear the least bit motivated to change his behavior.

"What's the big deal?" he asks with a look of defiance.

In response to this question, poor performers launched into lectures or threats. Positive deviants took a different path.

Or perhaps the coworker suggests that he faced an ability barrier:

"I tried, but, dude, I couldn't figure out how to use the tracking software."

In this case, the majority of people you see in action immediately jumped in and showed their colleagues what to do. Positive deviants weren't so quick to leap in with an answer.

On occasion, the coworker who had let them down dug in and became defensive, even disrespectful.

"Who died and left you in charge?"

With the majority, out came newer and even more pedantic lectures. Not so with positive deviants.

Skill by skill, our research team identified the insights and actions of those who routinely succeeded in the face of failure and then combined them into a training program that we used to teach accountability to hundreds of thousands of individuals worldwide. Eventually, in an effort to share these best practices with as many people as possible, we wrote this book.

BUT WILL IT WORK FOR ME?

After decades of tireless research, we have now identified about two-dozen accountability skills that, when used at the right time and delivered in the right fashion, separated positive deviants from everyone else. The questions remaining were (1) when taught, would people actually use the skills, and (2) if they did, would doing so yield better results?

The impact of teaching others the actions of positive deviants has been astounding. Of course, many people simply read a few passages from our work and walk away, changing nothing. Others make a feeble attempt to employ a skill or two, and to nobody's surprise, they too fail to improve. But when individuals (or even entire work groups or organizations) read, practice, and routinely use the best skills modeled by positive deviants, the gains have been enormous.

For instance, after we spent a year teaching best practices at the manufacturing plant where accountability was reported to have been lost, people started dealing with infractions in a direct and professional way, and profitability increased by over $40 million a year. When asked how this had taken place, the plant manager explained, "Our leaders now talk early on and solve problems before they grow out of control—and they do so in a way that not only solves the problem but also strengthens the relationship."

After completing our first project in the "land of no accountability," we worked in dozens of other organizations where we were able to track the specific relationship between holding accountability discussions and key performance indicators. Here are a few of our findings taken from VitalSmarts case studies:

- Hospitals that influence employees to embrace better ways of holding each other accountable for protocol infractions, such as failing to wash on the way in and out of patients' rooms, routinely move from the typical 70 percent compliance rate to nearly a perfect score. (On two occasions, the post-training scores were so high that compliance monitors doubted the results, repeated the analysis, and found that indeed, after being taught specific methods and scripts for dealing with protocol violations, hand-washing conformity reached nearly 100 percent.)

- After turning the use of crucial accountability skills into new norms for employees of a large telecom company, we found that an increase of 18 percent in the use of the skills corresponded with over 40 percent improvement in productivity.

- When an IT group improved crucial accountability practices by 22 percent, quality improved over 30 percent, productivity climbed almost 40 percent, and costs plummeted almost 50 percent, all while employee satisfaction swelled 20 percent.

- A project with a large defense contractor revealed that for each 1 percent increase in the use of the company's crucial accountability skills, there was a $1,500,000 gain in productivity. Nine months after beginning the training, employees improved 13 percent. You do the math.

- Perhaps the most interesting finding came in the form of personal career success. We learned that in order to find people who were good at holding others accountable, we simply needed to ask leaders who their most valued employees were. Almost without exception the top-valued employees selected by the leaders were positive deviants who had learned how to hold others accountable. Learn how to hold others accountable, learn how to bring predictability and trust into an organization, and you'll be counted as one of your company's most valued assets.

So if you want to peer out into the distant and murky future, stand on the shoulders of giants. If you want to learn the skills routinely employed by individuals who effectively hold others accountable—and equally important, enjoy the results that come from creating a culture of accountability—stand on the shoulders of positive deviants. We (the authors) have seen enormous benefits in our own lives as we've worked to turn insights gleaned from brilliant communicators into personal, lifelong habits.

ONE FINAL NOTE

We've taken the skills demonstrated by positive deviants and fashioned them into a Crucial Accountability skill set that provides direction for the rest of this book. The skill set provides a pathway for navigating accountability discussions before, during, and after the interaction takes place. It also helps match action to circumstance, leading to a thoughtful, response-driven conversation rather than the rote repeating of actions that come to mind after a lifetime of observing bad examples.

Have we piqued your interest?

It's time to learn and embrace the skills of those talented positive deviants out there and infuse our families, work groups, companies, and communities with the comforting predictability and relationship-affirming trust that come with accountability.

Part One

Work on Me First

What to Do Before an Accountability Crucial Conversation

When we approach an accountability discussion, it's important to know that we must work on ourselves first. We can't go in determined to "fix everyone else" and expect to get the results we're really after. We can only actually ever change ourselves.

That being said, remember that asking others to account for their actions lives and dies on the words people choose and the way people deliver them. Those words, and particularly the way they are delivered, live and die on what people think before they open their mouths. No amount of preparation can save a conversation if the person who brings up the failed promise isn't in the right frame of mind. Here's how those who master accountability discussions make sure their thoughts are in order before they put their mouths in gear:

- They make sure they are conversing about the right problems (Chapter 1, "Choose *What* and *If*").

- They make sure that the thoughts rushing around in their heads—their facts, stories, and emotions—help them see the other person as a person rather than a villain. They learn to control their strong emotions by revisiting the stories that caused them (Chapter 2, "Master My Stories").

1

> *I made a Freudian slip last night. I called my husband by the name of my first boyfriend. It was embarrassing.*
>
> *I did the same sort of thing. I meant to say to my husband, "Please pass the potatoes," but I said, "Die, loser; you've ruined my life!"*

Choose *What* and *If*

How to Know What *Conversation to Hold and* If *You Should Hold It*

Problems rarely come in tiny boxes—certainly not the issues we care about. Those come in giant bundles. For instance, your boss promises you a raise and then recants. This is the second time he's promised you something only to go back on the promise, except this time he dropped the bomb in a meeting, and so you couldn't complain on the spot. When you stopped him in the hallway to bring up the issue, he told you that he was in a hurry and said you should "stop being insensitive to my time demands." You asked if you could talk later, and he said, "Hey, I didn't get the money I deserved either."

Let's try a home example. Your in-laws just walked in unannounced while you were eating dinner. You've talked to them about giving you a heads-up, particularly if they plan on dropping in at dinnertime, and they still prance in on a whim. What problem do you address?

You don't have enough food to go around. That could be easy to discuss. They've repeatedly promised they would notify you but are constantly breaking that agreement and losing your trust. That is likely to be hard to bring up. Finally, after turning down your invitation to join you at the table, they pout and whimper in the corner. That could be *really* difficult to confront.

In each of these cases, you're left with two questions that you have to answer before you open your mouth: *What?* and *If?* First, *what* violation or violations should you actually address? How do you dismantle a bundle of accountability problems into its component parts and choose the one you want to discuss? You have a lot to choose from, and you can't talk about them all, at least not in one sitting. Second, you have to decide *if* you're going to say anything. Do you speak up and run the risk of causing a whole new set of problems, or do you remain silent and run the risk of never solving the problem?

Let's take these two questions one at a time. We'll deal with the *if* question once we've resolved the *what* question.

CHOOSING *WHAT*

The question of what you should discuss may be the most important concept we cover in this book. When problems come in complicated bundles, and they often do, it's not always easy to know which problem or problems to address.

For example, a teenage daughter swears to her father she'll be home from her first big date by midnight but doesn't come home until 1 a.m. Here's the pressing question: What problem should he discuss? "That's easy," you say. "She was late." True, that's one way to describe the problem.

Here are several other ways: She broke a promise. She violated her father's trust. She drove her father insane with fear that she had been killed in a car wreck. She purposely and willfully disobeyed a family rule. She openly defied her father in an effort to break free of parental control. She was getting even with her father for grounding her the weekend before. She knew it would drive her father bonkers if she stayed out late with a guy who sports a dozen face perforations, and so she did that.

Although it's true that the daughter walked in the door 60 minutes after curfew, this may not be the exact and only problem her father wants to discuss. Here's the added danger: if he selects the wrong problem from this lengthy list of possible problems and handles it well, he may be left with the impression that he's done the right thing. However, if you want to follow the footsteps of our positive deviants, you have to identify and deal with the right problem, or it will never go away. This still leaves us with this question: What is the right problem?

Signs That You're Dealing with the Wrong Problem
Your Solution Doesn't Get You What You Really Want

To get a feel for how to choose the right problem, let's look at an actual case we recently uncovered during a training session for school principals. It's from a grade school principal's experience. During recess a teacher notices the following interaction. Two second-grade girls are playing on the monkey bars. As Maria pushes Sarah to hurry her along, Sarah shouts, "Don't you ever touch me again, you dirty little Mexican!" Maria counters with, "At least I'm not a big fatty!" This is the precipitating event.

The principal calls the children's parents, describes what took place, and explains that the school will be disciplining them. Maria's parents are fine with the idea and thank the principal, and that's the end of the discussion. Sarah's mother takes a different approach. She asks, "Exactly what form of discipline will each child receive?" The principal explains that the discipline will suit the nature of the offense.

The next day Sarah's mother shows up unannounced, catches the principal in the hallway, and proclaims in loud and harsh tones that she doesn't want the school to discipline her daughter. She'll take care of the discipline on her own. The principal explains that the school is bound by policy to take action. In fact, tomorrow Sarah will be separated from her friends during lunch and required to take her meal in the media room under the supervision of a teacher's aide. That's the prescribed discipline. Sarah's mother then announces that tomorrow she'll be picking up her daughter for a private mommy-daughter lunch at a nearby restaurant.

There are several problems in this scenario. When the principals in the training session hear about the incident, many become emotional. "That's an easy one to figure out," some suggest. "You turn it over to the district discipline committee. Besides, since there are racial issues involved here, you could get the mother in trouble for interfering." Of course, the goal here isn't to cause the mother grief, so what should the principal do?

As the principals settle down to discuss the problem in earnest, they bring to the surface an assortment of issues: "First, there's the problem of meddling. She has no right to ask about the other child's discipline. It's a private matter." "No, the bigger issue is that she is demanding to take away the school's right to discipline. That's simply unacceptable." "Plus the kid's going to be rewarded with a special lunch instead of being punished. Who wants that?" "How about the fact that the mother is rude and manipulative? That can't be good."

Finally, one of the assistant principals brings up an issue that everyone seems to think is important: "I'm worried that the parent and the school won't be partnering in solving the problem. I'd want to work with the mother to come up with a plan jointly. Otherwise, she might begin to characterize the school officials as the enemy, and the child will soon agree."

Once this important issue is highlighted as the main problem, a discussion can be held to resolve it, and the principal can get what it is he or she really wants: a working partnership with the parent that will help benefit the child. Solutions to any of the other problems would not have accomplished this, and people would have remained frustrated.

So take note: if the solution you're applying doesn't get you the results you really want, it's likely you're dealing with the wrong problem entirely.

You're Constantly Discussing the Same Issue

Before we deal with the aggressive mother, let's look at another problem. This time you're working with the owner of a real estate firm in a rural community.

"The woman who works the front desk is constantly coming to work late," the owner explains.

"Have you talked to her?" you ask.

"Repeatedly" is the response.

"And then what happens?" you continue.

"She's on time for a few days, maybe even a week, and then she starts coming in late again."

"Then what do you say to her?"

"I tell her that she's late and that I don't like it."

This situation presents a terrific example of what separates accountability experts from everyone else. The owner has the courage to converse with the desk clerk. That separates him from the worst. However, the fact that he returns to the same problem each time puts him far below top performers. This is an indication that there is some other infraction that needs to be discussed: the front desk clerk isn't living up to her commitments, she's disrespecting company policy, etc.

> ### Groundhog Day
>
> When people repeatedly violate an expectation, those who are the best at identifying and then confronting the deviation redefine each instance with each new infraction. They don't live the wretched life of Phil Connors, the weatherman in the movie *Groundhog Day*. Those who observe repeated infractions and discuss each new instance as if it were the first one live the same problem (the same day) over and over, and nothing ever changes. Accountability experts never live Groundhog Day. The first time a person is late, she's late; the second time, she's failed to live up to her promise; the third time she's starting down the road to discipline, etc.

In summary, if you find yourself having the same accountability discussion over and over again, it's likely there's another, more important violation you need to address.

You're Getting Increasingly Upset

As you continue your conversation with the realtor, you say, "Obviously, the fact that your clerk comes in late is the behavior that catches your attention, and that's what you talk to her about. But what is the real issue here?"

"I'm not exactly sure. I do know that it's starting to bug me a lot—more than it probably should."

"Are you becoming more upset because the problem's escalating?"

"Not really," the broker responds hesitantly.

Finally, you ask, "When you're angry enough to complain to your wife, coworkers, or best friend about this repeated infraction, how do you describe it?"

A light goes on in the broker's eyes as he excitedly states, "It's killing me that she's taking advantage of our relationship. She's my neighbor, she's helped me out a lot, and now she doesn't do what I ask because she knows that I won't discipline her since we're good friends. At least that's how it feels to me."

That's the violated expectation the broker needs to confront. He's becoming increasingly upset with each instance because he's never dealt with the issue that is bothering him. Being late is the frozen tip floating above the chilly waters. Taking advantage of a friendship is the iceberg itself.

Confronting the Right Issue

As you can see from these examples, learning how to get at the gist of an infraction requires time and practice. Feeling pressured by time constraints and hyped up by emotions, most people miss the real deal. It takes grade school assistant principals 20 minutes or more to discuss the assortment of challenges presented in the case of the aggressive mother. In fact, most never come to the realization that it's the lack of cooperation that they probably ought to discuss. Many can't get past their emotional reaction. They want to stick it to the feisty mother, and, frankly, that's exactly what many would do.

Along a similar vein, most parents who pace the floor nervously as a teenage daughter breaks curfew can't see beyond the hands of the clock, when in truth what really has them concerned is the fact that the girl didn't have the courtesy to call them, let them know she'd be late, and bring a merciful end to their tortured worrying. Many don't even realize that this is what is troubling them.

The ability to reduce an infraction to its bare essence takes patience, a sense of proportion, and precision. First, you have to take the time to unbundle the problem. People are often in too much of a hurry to do this. Their emotions propel them to move quickly, and speed rarely leads to careful thought. Second, while sorting through the issues, you have to decide what is bothering you the most. If you don't, you'll end up going after either the wrong target or too many targets. Third, you have to be concise. You have to distill the issue to a single sentence. Lengthy descriptions of violated expectations only obscure the real issue. If you can't reduce a violation to a clear sentence before you talk, the issue almost never becomes more understandable and focused as a conversation unfolds.

Helpful Tools to Get to the Right Conversation

Let's say that despite your best efforts, you keep returning to the same infraction. Your emotions are getting worse, not better, and in retrospect you believe that you're choosing to talk about what's easy, convenient, or obvious but not what's important. In short, you have every reason to believe that you're repeatedly dealing with the wrong issue. How do you turn this bad habit around? To hit the right target, use the following tools.

Think CPR

This acronym can help give direction to an accountability discussion as well as eliminate Groundhog Day. The first time an infraction occurs, talk about the *content*, what just happened: "You drank too much at the luncheon, became inebriated, started talking too loud, made fun of our clients, and embarrassed the company." The content of a violated expectation typically deals with a single event—the here and now.

The next time the infraction occurs, talk *pattern*, what has been happening over time: "This is the second time this has occurred. You agreed it wouldn't happen again, and I'm concerned that I can't count on you to keep a promise." Pattern issues acknowledge that problems have histories and that histories make a difference. Frequent and continued violations affect the other person's predictability and eventually harm respect and trust.

Warning: It's easy to miss the pattern and get sucked into debating content. For instance, your boss repeatedly leaves your agenda items to the end of the meeting—meaning that they typically get abbreviated or dropped altogether. You've spoken with her about it before. This time when you bring it up, she explains how full the agenda was and how you need to be more flexible about urgent issues. If you give in to that explanation, you've missed the point. Your concern is not today's meeting (the content issue); it's the long-standing pattern. Sometimes the pattern sneaks up on you, and a new issue arises. You point out the problem, and the other person begins to either rant or pout, something that's starting to happen a lot in your conversations with him or her. It's becoming a pattern. Accountability savants notice this pattern of behavior and find ways to address it before moving back to the original topic.

As the problem continues, talk about *relationship*, what's happening to us. Relationship concerns are far bigger than either the content or the pattern. The issue is not that other people have repeatedly broken promises; it's that the string of disappointments has caused you to lose trust in them: you're beginning to doubt their competency and doubt their promises, and this is affecting the way you treat one another: "This is starting to put a strain on how we work together. I feel as if I have to nag you to keep you in line, and I don't like doing that. I guess my fear is that I can't trust you to keep the agreements you make."

If your real concern is around the *relationship* and you discuss only the pattern of behavior, you're likely to find yourself feeling dissatisfied with the outcome. Even worse, you're likely to experience Groundhog Day: you'll have the same conversation again later. To understand the various kinds of content, pattern, and relationship issues that routinely pop up during accountability discussions, consider the following two factors: consequences and intentions. Each provides a distinct method for first unbundling and then placing a priority on violated expectations.

Unbundling

Consequences

Accountability issues are almost never contained in the behavior of the offender. They're much more likely to be a function of what happens afterward. The problem lies in the consequences. For example, a staff specialist who works for you has promised to complete a financial analysis by noon. She miscalculates how long it will take and delivers the job to you three hours late.

The errant behavior, being late, is not the problem. What follows is. The fact that you might lose a client is what really bothers you. Or maybe it's the fact that this is the third time this person has let you down and you're beginning to wonder if you can count on her. Or perhaps it's the fact that you now may have to watch this person more closely, costing you precious time and making her feel micromanaged. Each of these responses is a consequence of the original act and helps unbundle the problem.

When you want to clarify the focus of your accountability discussion, stop and ask yourself, "What are the consequences to me? To our relationship? To the task? To other stakeholders?" Analyzing the consequences helps you determine what is most important to discuss.

Intentions

Let's move the analysis in another direction. A fellow you work with is causing you a problem. He cheerfully promised to format a report you created, and then, instead of giving it to you, he handed it directly to your boss. What was he thinking? Actually, you have a theory. You believe that his intentions were selfish (he was trying to take credit); at least, this is the conclusion you've drawn.

Let's be clear about this. You've drawn this conclusion not as a thoughtless knee-jerk reaction, as is often the case, but as the result of mounting evidence. You've examined the action, you've weighed the particulars, and you are starting to believe the person's intentions are indeed bad. When this happens, the behavior isn't the problem, at least not the big one. What came before the person acted is the challenge here, at least in your mind. It's the issue you ought to discuss. You have to talk about intentions.

The good news is that we address intentions all the time. Consider the father who was upset with his daughter for coming in late because she was punishing him for having grounded her. It wasn't the fact that she had been late that made him upset—at least not totally—it was her perceived intention that was giving him fits: "She's doing it on purpose just to cause me grief." The realtor believed that the front desk clerk was intentionally playing on their friendship to get away with coming in late. Once again, it was her perceived intent that bothered him.

Whether the father and the realtor are correct in their assessments will remain unknown until they hold an accountability discussion and share their suspicions. Of course, deciding how they'll confront such a delicate issue isn't easy. These are invisible motives we're talking about. We're drawing conclusions about another person's unseen intent. (We'll discuss the common stories we tell ourselves in later chapters.) Nevertheless, the conclusions the two have drawn about others' underlying intent has them bothered, and these are the issues they'll need to talk about eventually.

Prioritizing
Ask What You Do and Don't Want

As you begin to unbundle the component parts of a violated expectation—examining the precipitating intentions and the consequences—the list of component parts can grow so large that you may not know where to begin. What's the "real" issue, or at least the most important one?

The best tool for choosing from the host of possible infractions is to ask what you really want and don't want. And since you're talking to another person, you ought to ask what you want for yourself, for the other person, and for the relationship. If you don't think about all three of these essential aspects, one may take a backseat, and you won't solve your most important issue.

Consider the case of the two second-grade girls. Most people struggle with what to say to Sarah's mother until someone asks: "What do you want to have happen with Sarah? What don't you want to have happen?" You do want Sarah to be disciplined. You don't want to start a battle with her mother and make choices that limit Sarah's educational options. You don't want to send her to a new school just to show her mother who's in charge.

As far as you yourself are concerned, you want to be able to hold Sarah accountable. Policy demands that you take action, and even if you could look the other way, you'd be giving tacit approval to a nasty behavior. You don't want that. When it comes to the relationship, you want to be able to collaborate with Sarah's mother to come up with the proper type of discipline. You don't want the daughter to receive mixed messages. So what do you say? What is the problem you want to discuss? "I'm afraid we're sending Sarah the wrong message when we argue over the form the discipline should take."

To decide what to confront:

- Think CPR—content, pattern, and relationship.

- Expand the list of possible issues by considering consequences and intent.

- Choose from the list by asking what you do and don't want: for yourself, others, and the relationship.

An Application

Let's apply these concepts to a real case. Your two preteen kids were invited to go to a drive-in movie with their friends who live down the street. You gave them permission to stay up late and you popped popcorn for them, and your children are now so excited that they can hardly see straight. Then the parents who will be taking the kids to the movie drive up to your house in their pickup truck. Their two children are seated in the truck bed, and your kids quickly join them. You have a strict family rule about not riding in the back of a pickup, particularly one that will be driving at freeway speed to get to the movie. Your spouse feels as strongly about the safety issue as you do.

You start to raise your safety concerns, and your neighbor calls you a "fussbudget" and a "worrywart." Before you can respond, your spouse cuts you off and tries to smooth over the issue by saying to the father who is driving, "You're going to be extra careful, right? Those kids in the back are pretty precious cargo!" The driver says not to worry and pulls off as your kids squeal in delight.

You're furious. What do you say to your spouse? Your first inclination is to talk about the danger. But that ship has sailed, well, sort of rumbled, off into the sunset. Although you'll return to the issue later, when your kids are around (they're aware of the dangers of getting into the truck), you think that maybe you should talk about the fact that this is the second time your spouse has backed off on a family value under pressure. That's a new challenge—backing off a value (not just safety)—and it's a pattern. Then again, what really has you miffed is the fact that your spouse cut you off as you were raising the safety issue with your neighbor. You think that your spouse's intention was cock-eyed. It was more important to look "cool" than to ensure the safety of your children.

As you think about it, you ask yourself what you want and don't want. You want the kids to be safe—that's a given—but once again, you'll talk about that issue as a group. You want to be able to express concerns without being cut off or dismissed. You want your spouse to be able to talk about the issue without making you feel attacked. You don't want the discussion to turn into a fight. As far as your relationship is concerned, you want to stand as a unified front when it comes to safety. And then you put your finger on the real kicker. The pattern you are concerned about is your spouse unintentionally taking away your vote in these key decisions. Yes, that's it! It's when your spouse announces a decision publicly without ensuring that you're in agreement.

You decide to talk about making commitments (especially those that deviate from values such as safety) without each other's buy-in. You want to find a way to always stand together when faced with outside pressures, and safety is certainly not an exception. That's the big issue.

DECIDE *IF*

Let's move on to the *if* question. You've unbundled the violation, picked the issue you care about the most, and reduced it to a clear sentence, and now you're ready. You're going to hold an accountability discussion with the other person. Or are you? The mere fact that you've identified the problem you'd like to discuss doesn't mean you should discuss it. Sometimes it's better to consider the consequences before deciding whether to bring up the issue.

For instance, your teenage son walks in the door with his hair cut in a Mohawk. He loves it. You hate it. He thinks it's all the rage. You think it's a sign of rebellion. Do you lay down the law or back off? Maybe you're out of touch with what is normal and what isn't. Haranguing your son until he opts for a new style might do little more than widen the rift that seems to be growing between the two of you. Maybe you shouldn't say anything. Maybe you should expand your zone of acceptance.

Let's consider an example from work. Your boss is combative in meetings. She verbally attacks arguments by raising her voice and labeling ideas "stupid" or "naive" and often looks disgusted. She also disagrees with almost everything and cuts people off midsentence. At first her tactics bothered you, but you came to appreciate the fact that at least it was clear where she stood on issues. Therefore, you said nothing. Today she questioned your loyalty and insulted you in front of your peers. That was going too far. Maybe you should say something. Maybe you should shrink your zone of acceptance.

As these examples demonstrate, there are no simple rules that dictate which violated expectations are trivial, which are consequential, and which you should deal with. Usually when someone breaks a promise, you talk about it—circumstances demand that you talk, and you do—but not always. So what are the rules?

When It's Clearly a Broken Promise

In organizations there are reports, goals, performance indicators, quality scorecards, budget variances, and a boatload of other metrics that clearly show a difference between what was expected and what was delivered. These failed promises represent clear opportunities to hold an accounting. And since they're routine, they're probably fairly easy to discuss.

At home there are also clear indicators: "You promised me we'd go out to dinner." "You told me you would be home for my birthday." These too are routine issues that are easily discussed.

When It's Unclear and Iffy

But what if the infractions are ambiguous or if discussing them could get you in trouble? You're not sure if the infraction is a problem and if bringing up the issue might lead to a raging battle, a harmed relationship, a lost job, or something equally frightening.

How do you know if you should address broken promises that are not so clear and not so promising?

To answer this all-important *if* question, let's divide the challenge into two camps: First, how do you know if you're not speaking up when you should? Second, how do you know if you are speaking up when you shouldn't?

Not Speaking When You Should

Let's start with a simple premise. As was evidenced in our line-cutting research and the numerous studies that followed, more often than not, we don't speak up when we should. Sure, sometimes we bring up an issue at the wrong time or in the wrong way, but that's not the predominant mistake made in most families and companies. Going to silence is the prominent issue in these situations.

To help diagnose whether you're clamming up when you should be speaking up, ask the following four questions:

- Am I acting out my concerns?
- Is my conscience nagging me?
- Am I choosing the certainty of silence over the risk of speaking up?
- Am I telling myself that I'm helpless?

Am I Acting Out My Concerns?

Let's say you've observed a broken commitment at work. Several members of the technical support team aren't keeping an eight-to-five work schedule. Instead, they're working flextime. They often arrive late and then work past closing. This bugs you because they agreed to stick to the posted schedule.

After thinking about it, you decide that maybe being a stickler isn't such a good idea. They're putting in the hours, and there's no need to rock the boat. You're still bugged because they broke their word and it feels like they're acting like prima donnas, but you're not going to say a word.

Holding your tongue probably isn't going to work in this case. If the broken commitment is really bothering you, you're unlikely to be a good enough actor to hide your feelings. You may try to choke your feelings down, but eventually they'll bubble up to the surface in unhealthy ways. If you don't talk it out, you'll act it out.

An actor named John LaMotta taught us this concept. We had hired him to play the role of a manager in a training video we were producing. During rehearsals he kept turning the rather harmless opening line into an attack. Later we learned that he had assumed that the person he was working with was a "dipstick" because he hadn't done his job. Consequently, no matter how we directed John (telling him to soften his delivery, drop the anger, etc.), he treated the fellow with disdain. John didn't stray from the written script, but his negative assumptions found their way into his nonverbal behavior: first his tone, then a smirk, then a raised fist, and so forth. When the director finally told John that the fellow was a hard worker whom everyone liked, John delivered his lines spot-on. He couldn't change his actions until he changed his mind.

Paul Ekman,[1] a scholar who has studied facial expressions and emotions for 30 years, came to the same conclusion. When people try to hide their feelings or "put on" an emotion, Ekman found they use different groups of muscles than they use to express authentic feelings. For example, authentic smiles of joy involve the muscles surrounding the eyes; false or social smiles bypass the eyes completely. And other people can tell. You can't hide your real emotions.

There's more. When you observe a broken commitment, feel bad about it, and then decide to say nothing, your feelings don't manifest themselves only in your facial expressions and other nonverbal behaviors; they also escape in the form of biting sarcasm, cutting humor, or surprising non sequiturs. For instance, while seated across from his mother at the dinner table, a 29-year-old chronically unemployed son politely tells her that she has "a hunk of lasagna" on her chin. Mom responds with, "Oh, yeah? When I was your age, I had two jobs." Guess what has been annoying her?

When you've gone silent, but your body language keeps sending out hostile signals or you're dropping hints or relying on sarcasm, you probably ought to speak up.

What Are We Thinking?

Why do we ever set aside pressing problems—hoping they'll somehow get better? It's like finding a tub of rancid cottage cheese in the fridge, setting it on the kitchen counter for a couple of days, and then thinking, "Gee, I wonder if it'll taste any better now."

Is My Conscience Nagging Me?

Sometimes you don't hold others accountable because you feel isolated. You see a problem but fear that you're the only one who cares. No one else shows signs of anxiety. "Now what am I supposed to do?" you wonder. "Why aren't my healthcare colleagues concerned that we're not washing our hands long enough?" "How come my fellow accountants are looking the other way when our biggest client violates standard practices?" "How come my neighbors, spouse, and kids don't think riding in the bed of a pickup is dangerous?" Even though you're worried—your conscience is nagging you a little—you say nothing.

As we suggested in the Introduction, the fact that people often remain silent despite their best judgment has been studied extensively. In addition to the studies we cited, Solomon Asch[2] created conditions in which people wouldn't just remain silent when they believed they were at odds with their peers; they actually lied rather than disagree with them. Stanley Milgram[3] replaced peers with authority figures and was able to manipulate the subjects to do more than lie. He got people to shock others to the point where they worried that they might have killed the other persons rather than disagree with the individual in the white lab jacket.

Peer pressure coupled with formal authority can compel people to act against their best judgment. Here's how it affects accountability discussions: if social pressure can cause people to lie, it can certainly drive people to silence. Pay attention to a nagging conscience—it may be indicating a conversation that you need to step up to.

> When you've gone to silence and your conscience is nagging you, you probably ought to speak up.

Am I Choosing the Certainty of Silence over the Risk of Speaking Up?

When it comes to deciding whether we're going to speak up, we kid ourselves into making the same mental math errors. We choose the certainty of what is currently happening to us (no matter how awful it may be) over the uncertainty of what might happen if we said something. This of course drives us to silence, quietly embracing the devil we know, when there's a good chance that we really should have spoken up. Here's how this insidious dynamic works.

When we're trying to figure out if we should speak up, we often envision a horrific failure and immediately decide to go to silence. Then we look for reasons to justify the choice to say nothing. Our reasoning takes place in the following way. We first ask ourselves, "Can I succeed in this conversation?" We don't ask, "Should I try?" Instead, we ask, "Can I succeed?" When the answer to the internal query is a resounding no, we decide that we shouldn't try.

Accountability experts take the opposite approach. Only after they've decided that the conversation should be held do they ask the question, "How can I do this? Better still, how can I do this well?" If we reverse the order, starting with *can* and not *should*, we almost always sell out. We decide to clam up and then justify our inaction.

Our two favorite silence-driving math tricks are (1) downplaying the cost of not speaking and (2) exaggerating the cost of expressing our views.

Downplaying the Cost of Not Speaking

Here's how we minimize in our own minds the cost of continuing to tolerate the status quo. First, we look exclusively at what's happening to us in the moment rather than at the total effect. A professor is boring, unfair, and outdated, but why rock the boat? We'll survive, right? Never mind the fact that thousands of students will be affected over the next two decades of that professor's career.

Second, we underestimate the severity of the existing circumstances because we become inured to the consequences we're suffering. With time and constant exposure we come to believe that our wretched conditions are common and therefore acceptable. We continue to work for authoritarian bosses, stay married to people who physically and mentally abuse us, and work alongside people who ignore and insult us because we tell ourselves that it's not really that bad. It's just how things are.

Third, as was suggested earlier, we can't see our own bad behavior when we fail to maintain silence. For example, we think we're silently suffering under the thumb of a micromanager. In actuality, we act offended when the boss asks for details. We say we know how to do the job, cutting her off when she tries to offer a suggestion. We defiantly choose to do something our way. We miss the fact that our own behavior has degraded. In this case we don't merely downplay the cost of silence—we miss it entirely.

Exaggerating the Cost of Expressing Our Views
Let's look at how we routinely overestimate the costs we might experience if we did talk about a broken promise. Human beings are downright gifted when it comes to conjuring up bad things that just might happen to them. In fact, when contemplating what we may be setting into action by opening our mouths, we often imagine (and then get obsessed about) appalling outcomes no matter how unlikely they may be. When we trump up a horrible chain of events, we use lots of "and" thinking, only the wrong kind of "and" thinking. Here's how it works:

> *The boss has asked us all to chip in 20 bucks to buy a present for a vice president we don't even know. That's a certainty, and it's bad. None of us want to do it. But if I speak up, I won't win the argument, and I'll still have to come up with the money, and my boss will despise me, and I'll lose my job, and my wife will leave me.*

We lose all sense of reality when we fixate on the horrific possibilities that might befall us. The severity of the possible outcomes distorts our view of the probabilities. If an unlikely outcome is bad enough, we often describe it as a certainty rather than a possibility.

Perhaps the largest error we make in exaggerating the cost of confronting an issue stems from the erroneous belief that the existing world always punishes people who are naive enough to speak their minds. We've watched people speak up and get punished for their honesty and find it hard to imagine any other possibility. In fact, when the authors suggest in public forums that this book teaches people how to talk to almost anyone no matter how touchy and powerful that person may be—and with good results—people think we're fooling ourselves: "Maybe the pumpkin wagon you just fell off allows you to speak honestly and boldly to the driver, but our driver carries a whip and loves to use it."

At first we wondered if the skills we had seen demonstrated so often wouldn't work in certain instances, and so we started asking, "Are you saying that there is nobody in your company who could talk about this particular issue or person and get away with it?" After an awkward pause, someone would name an individual who didn't have the position power that granted him or her the right to speak but somehow found ways to talk quite frankly and not get into trouble.

When you've gone to silence and are trying way too hard to convince yourself that you've done the right thing, you might want to examine whether you are intentionally minimizing the cost of not speaking up and exaggerating the risks of doing so. Did you *start* with a desire not to speak up and back into a justification, or did you arrive there after careful consideration? Learn to notice the difference, and you'll do a much better job of deciding if you should talk to someone about an issue.

Am I Telling Myself That I'm Helpless?

At the heart of most decisions to stay quiet, even though we're currently suffering, lies the fear that we won't be able to make a difference. We believe that either other people or the circumstances themselves make the problem insoluble. That puts the issue out of our control. It's not us; it's them: "Have you ever tried to talk to that guy? He's a maniac!" "Have you ever attempted to tell a senior executive that she doesn't really know how to do her job? Like that's going to work."

The truth is that many accountability discussions fail not because others are bad and wrong but because we handle them poorly. It's our fault. We decide to step up to a failed promise and subtly attack the other person. He or she then gets hooked, and we're now in a heated battle. Naturally, we see the other person getting hooked but miss the part we played in escalating the problem by doing such a shoddy job of bringing it up in the first place.

We're like the young boy who refused to see his role in an argument by explaining to his mother, "It all started when he hit me back!"

Even when we do see the role we're playing in a problem by owning up to the fact that our accountability skills aren't that great, we often act as if we were as talented as we're ever going to be. We've peaked; we'll never get better. We make this assumption because most of us aren't exactly students of social influence. We've spent more time memorizing the capitals of Europe than we have examining the intricacies of human interaction. We rarely think of accountability skills as something that a person should and can learn through actual study. But as this book asserts, these skills can be learned and improved.

When you've gone to silence because you're afraid you're not skilled enough to have an accountability discussion, your assessment may be correct. If this is the case, enhance your skills. There's no use suffering forever. Be careful not to let fear taint your judgment. You may have the skills to deal with a particular issue but are letting your fear keep you from speaking up. When you're thinking about going to silence, ask yourself if you're copping out rather than making a reasoned choice.

Responding to the Signs

Let's summarize the clues that you're hastily going to silence and explore what to do with them. Telltale signs that you should be speaking and not clamming up include the following four:

- *Sign 1.* You're acting out your feelings. You think you're suffering silently, but you're not. To spot this mistake, ask yourself the following: "Am I really expanding my zone of acceptance, or am I actually upset and sending out a barrage of unhealthy signals? Are others getting hooked?" If this is the case, you're probably not suffering silently but are acting out your concerns and making matters worse. Your nonverbal behavior is already speaking for you. Consider taking charge of the conversation instead.

- *Sign 2.* Your conscience is nagging you. You keep telling yourself that it's okay to say nothing—besides, other people aren't saying a word—but you know in your gut that you need to say something. Listen to that voice. It's telling you to step up to the plate. Take the internal prodding as a sign that your silence isn't warranted.

- *Sign 3.* You're downplaying the cost of not taking action (embracing the devil you know) while exaggerating the dangers of speaking up. You're trying way too hard to persuade yourself to stay away from an accountability discussion because you fear it will be painful. Don't confuse the question of whether the conversation will be difficult with the question of whether you should deal with it.

- *Sign 4.* You figure that nothing you do will help. Either others are impossible to talk to, or you've already achieved the height of your accountability prowess. In truth, the problem is less often that others are impossible to approach than that we aren't sure how to approach them. The authors have watched people deal with some of the most difficult problems and succeed because they knew what to say and how to say it. If you improve your skills—even just a little—you'll choose silence far less often and succeed far more routinely.

Speaking Up When You Shouldn't

Let's turn our attention to the other side of the *if* coin. You confront a problem that in retrospect you probably shouldn't have dealt with in the first place. This seems to contradict what we just discussed, but it's true. There are times when it's better not to bring up a problem or at least not to do so until you've done some preparatory work.

Often, when you've weighed the consequences of speaking up, it is a better option to remain silent. For example, you've had difficulty working with a certain vendor and the process could have been much cleaner, but you were working on a one-time-only project and probably won't ever see the vendor again. In this case, it may be better to avoid rehashing an issue that will never come up again.

Here's the biggest stumbling block: problem solving is never done in a vacuum. Every company and family has an unwritten history that indicates which infractions are appropriate to deal with and which ones a person should let slide. All expectations, contracts, protocols, policies, and promises aren't equally binding. Worse, in some organizations people aren't held accountable for delivering on any promises, or at least accountability is unpredictable.

Differentiate Yourself

Sometimes erratic approaches to accountability stem from the fact that leaders take the path of least resistance. It isn't fun to hold people accountable; besides, nobody's taught them much about it. Sometimes people hold back their concerns out of sympathy for the fact that everyone is assigned far more than he or she can ever do, and so it feels almost cruel to hold people accountable.

Whatever the underlying cause, if you're going to break from tradition and elevate a standard that had been nothing more than a rough guideline to a hard-and-fast law, people should know. You have to issue a fair warning. You have to reset others' expectations, and you have to do it in a way that doesn't look smug.

For example, one day Kerry, one of the authors of this book, put on his new Coast Guard dress uniform in preparation for standing watch. He was going to take his turn as the officer of the day (OD) at a training center in California where he had been newly assigned. He would be in charge of the watch.

The watch consisted of a couple of dozen "coasties" who had to remain on the base all night and "stand a post." They would sit in the barracks, motor pool, or boathouse and watch for any problems that might come up, including fires. Leaving one's post, Kerry had learned weeks earlier in officer training, could get a person brought up on charges.

Imagine Kerry's surprise later that evening when he caught wind that several of the men on duty were actually at the club chatting with their buddies rather than standing their posts and watching for whatever. Fortunately, before Kerry could march down and catch those fellows red-handed, leading to a great deal of pain and sorrow, a senior enlisted man took him aside and pointed out a couple of facts. First, lots of people on watch hung out at the club; nobody really cared. Second, several of Kerry's fellow officers were known to go down to the club and chat, throw darts, and otherwise turn a blind eye to the fact that some members of the duty crew weren't at their posts. If Mr. Patterson wanted to make a stink, there would not be a horde of adoring fans hoisting him on their shoulders to honor his vigilance.

What should Kerry do? He didn't like the idea of making rules and then not keeping them, and he certainly had the authority to write people up. However, if other officers had been turning a blind eye to regulations for a long time and now without notice Kerry, the new kid on the block, blindsided people with a charge of disobedience, it could seem unfair. The fact that you have legal standing doesn't mean that you'll gain the support of the larger community.

After seeking the counsel of his boss, Kerry decided to take the following tack. He wouldn't run, and he wouldn't blow the whistle (there was nobody to listen, and most people didn't care), and so he decided to strike a compromise. He let it be known that he appreciated the fact that other people had different opinions on the matter, but he didn't want people to leave their posts. When he was the OD, he would be checking the various posts to ensure that they were being watched. He then told a dozen or more opinion leaders about his stance and asked them to spread the word so that there wouldn't be any surprises. That was the end of the problem. Nobody left his post on Kerry's watch.

If you're going to speak up when others remain silent, if you're going to hold people to a standard that differs from that of the masses, get the word out. Send out a warning. Differentiate yourself from others. This is particularly wise advice for those moving into new positions of leadership, parents taking over blended families, etc.

No "Nanner-Nanner"

Over the years, as the authors have worked with thousands of leaders, they occasionally have run into people who are proud of the fact that they are the only ones who have the guts to hold people to quality guidelines, safety standards, cost-cutting goals, and the like. Others may remain quiet while quality crashes or costs spiral out of control, but not on their watch. Others may bolt at the first signs of resistance, but they hold the line.

With time we have come to understand that while being true to one's values may be noble, if you do so in a way that dishonors your peers (making fun of the less vigilant, bragging about your own commitment, etc.), you're upholding one value only to deny another: teamwork. Along a similar vein, parents who piously set a new standard, all the while making fun of a partner who isn't as discriminating as they are, do so at the peril of their children's mental health. Inconsistency breeds insecurity.

If you're going to differentiate yourself from your spouse or coworkers by holding people to a more rigid standard, don't be smug about it. Set expectations in a way that shows respect for people with different views. This may be a real test of your appreciation for diversity. You believe that people who hold individuals to a less rigid standard than you do are different—not spineless wimps who are slowly eating away at the very soul of civilization. There's a huge difference between saying "I'm going to ask you to do something even if others don't" and saying "I don't care what the other lily-livered losers are doing."

CHAPTER SUMMARY

Choose *What* and *If*

We've started with the principle "work on me first." We've learned that before we utter a word, we have to start by asking what accountability discussion to hold and if we should hold it.

What and *If*

- *What.* The first time someone violates an expectation, talk about the original action or the *content.* If the violation continues, talk about the *pattern.* As the impact spills over to how you relate to one another, talk about your *relationship.* To help pick the right level, explore what came after the behavior (the *consequences*) as well as what came before it (the *intent*). As the list of potential infractions expands, cut to the heart of the matter by asking what you really *do want* and *don't want*—for yourself, the other person, and the relationship.

- *If.* To determine if you're wrongly going to silence, ask four questions: "Am I acting it out?" "Is my conscience nagging me?" "Am I choosing the certainty of silence over the risk of speaking up?" "Am I telling myself that I'm helpless?" To determine if you're wrongly speaking up, ask if the social system will support your effort. If you are committed to speak up while others continue to say nothing, differentiate yourself.

What's Next?

Once you've decided to hold others accountable, you have to make sure that you yourself are in the right frame of mind. You have to work on yourself first. This isn't always easy, especially when the other person has let you down. There's a good chance that you'll charge in with an accusation. This takes us to the next chapter. Before you ever open your mouth, how do you tell a more complete and full story of what's going on—one that's more conducive to a healthy discussion than the all-too-common question, "What's wrong with those bozos?"

2

Master My Stories

How to Get Your Head Right Before Opening Your Mouth

Anyone who has ever held others accountable realizes that a person's behavior during the first few seconds of the interaction sets the tone for everything that follows. You have no more than a sentence or two to establish the climate. If you set the wrong tone or mood, it's hard to turn things around. In fact, a bad beginning might ensure a poor ending.

This can be troublesome, because when someone breaks a commitment or behaves badly, the last thing we're thinking about is the climate we're about to establish. More often than not, we're completely immersed in the details of what just happened. And if that doesn't consume all our time and attention, our emotions eat up anything that's left. Consider the following example.

HANG THE GEARHEADS!

Imagine that you're part of an overworked, stressed-out management team that's sitting around a table large enough to double as an airport runway, discussing what it'll take to finish a development project. The phone rings. The quality manager picks it up, carries on a heated discussion, and then slams the phone back onto its cradle.

"It's final assembly. The software we just completed is giving them fits," she says with a look typically associated with the act of biting the head off a chicken.

"Oh great! The software is glitchy!" shouts the vice president of development.

Within seconds the entire leadership team is complaining about the unorthodox, selfish, weird software testers. Then the team members arise as one and start marching toward the testing department. Since you've worked with this team for only a month, you aren't sure what's going on.

As the team members hustle down the hallway, the operations manager explains that the software is supposed to be tested and retested before it's sent on to final assembly. Otherwise, it often causes problems, and expensive ones at that.

"The stupid gearheads only have to run a simple testing package. That way they can catch problems early on and we never send software on to final assembly, where it can cause costly delays."

"Why didn't they run the tests?" you ask.

"That's what we're about to find out," answers the senior VP as the vein on his forehead swells to the size of a mop handle. He and the other leaders charge down the hall like a band of white-collar vigilantes, and you think to yourself, "This is about to turn ugly."

Behold, a Train Wreck

Obviously, this group has a checkered history with the people it's about to accost. The managers are feeling morally superior and are about to create a nasty scene. Of course, in many companies, interactions may not get that heated. The tone may be softer, the language less brutal, and the threats more veiled (less punitive folks rely more on cold stares, sarcasm, and pointed humor), but the results are probably the same. Employees fail to deliver on a promise, and the bosses jump to a conclusion and jump hard.

What makes these accountability discussions interesting is that the underlying cause doesn't really matter. If leaders start out with strong emotions, believing that they are on the moral high road, the interaction is likely to turn out badly for everyone regardless of the underlying cause.

The scene continues as the managers rush in like so many deputies preparing for a lynching. They catch the programmers checking out a "cool new website with a free game download" and then do what one might expect: They snarl at the guilty testers, call them unflattering names, threaten them with discipline, curse them, and pretty much throw a group hissy fit.

This ugly battle rages until the information technology manager, who just walked into the building, hears about what's happening to "his people" and rallies to the testers' defense. A full-fledged shouting match ensues. It's not long before the IT manager is accusing the rest of the management team of treating the programmers with disrespect, making false accusations, and using offensive language.

The managers are now so angry that they could spit. They've caught the weasels red-handed—they really had messed up—and their colleague, the IT manager, has the nerve to be pointing a finger at the management team. Has the world gone completely mad? It takes days for this incident to settle down, and everyone ends up with egg on his or her face. Everyone.

The Hazardous Half Minute

We used to call the first 30 seconds of an accountability discussion the hazardous half minute because the overall climate and eventual results are often set in place in seconds. We were wrong. The climate isn't set in the first 30 seconds; it just becomes *visible* in that time frame. We establish the climate the moment we assume that the other person is guilty and begin feeling angry and morally superior. It takes only a moment to send an accountability discussion down the wrong track, and it all takes place inside our heads. Here's what this looks like:

Another person violates a commitment, and, as a result, we're propelled to action. Here's the path we take: We see what that person did and then tell ourselves a story about *why* he or she did it, which leads to a feeling, which leads to our own actions. If the story is unflattering and the feeling is anger, adrenaline kicks in. Under the influence of adrenaline, blood leaves our brains to help support our genetically engineered response of "fight or flight," and we end up thinking with the brain of a reptile. We say and do dim-witted things.

Under these circumstances we come to some of the most ignorant conclusions imaginable. For instance, a fellow comes home from a long road trip and is feeling amorous, but his wife isn't. Soon he's pacing around and muttering to himself. Finally, here's the plan his blood-starved brain comes up with: "I've got it. I'll try to woo her with a sarcastic comment or two." Oddly enough, insensitive sarcasm doesn't seem to do anything to soften his wife's mood.

Consider the software development leaders. First came the observation: the software isn't working. Next came the story: the testers didn't run the final tests because they don't like doing them; in fact, they live in their own little world and don't care what happens to others. Then came the feeling of anger, followed by a fierce and futile attack. This entire path to action—the jump from observation, to story, to feeling, to action—takes but a moment and sets the tone for everything that follows.

THE PROBLEM: TELLING UGLY STORIES

Is it possible that everyday people with an IQ higher than that of a houseplant could be so hasty, judgmental, and unfair? Aren't most of us more careful, scientific, and thoughtful? In a word, no. We may not be as blatantly abusive as the managers in the software case, but when we face high-stakes problems, we're just as likely to come up with an unflattering story and act on it as if it were true.

Jumping to Conclusions and Making Assumptions

How can this be? During the 1950s and 1960s, scholars conducted a lengthy series of research projects known as attribution studies. Their goal was to learn how normal people determine the cause of a problem. To uncover the thought pattern, they provided subjects with descriptions of people engaging in socially unacceptable behavior (a woman steals cash from a coworker, a father yells at his children, a neighbor cuts in front of you in the checkout line) and then asked the subjects, "Why did that person do such a thing?"

It turns out that people aren't all that good at attributing causality accurately. We quickly jump to unflattering conclusions. The chief error we make is a simple one: we assume that people do what they do because of personality factors (mostly motivational) *alone*. Why did that woman steal from a coworker? She's dishonest. Why did that man yell at his children? He's mean.

Why did the programmers fail to conduct a test? They're arrogant, lazy, and selfish.

How can we be so simplistic and inaccurate? Most of the time human beings employ what is known as a dispositional rather than a situational view of others. We argue that people act the way they do because of uncontrollable personality factors (their disposition) as opposed to doing what they do because of forces in their environment (the situation).

We make this attribution error because when we look at others, we see their actions far more readily than we see the forces behind them. In contrast, when considering our own actions, we're acutely aware of the forces behind our choices. Consequently, we believe that others do bad things because of personality flaws whereas we do bad things because the devil made us do them.

In truth, people often enact behaviors they take no joy in because of social pressure, lack of other options, or any of a variety of forces that have nothing to do with personal pleasure. For example, the woman stole because she needed money to buy medicine for her children. Your neighbor cut in line at the market because he was tending to his two toddlers and didn't notice that he wasn't taking his turn. Your half cousin was hauled off to jail for holding up a convenience store partly because of greed; then again, maybe the slow and painful failure of his business contributed too.

The Fundamental Attribution Error

Assuming that others do contrary things because it's in their makeup or they actually enjoy doing them and then ignoring any other potential motivational forces is a mistake. Psychologists classify this mistake as an attribution error. And because it happens so consistently across people, times, and places, it gets a name all its own. It's called the *fundamental attribution error*.

Naturally, when we spot an infraction, we don't *always* conclude that the other person is bad and wrong and wants to make us suffer. For instance, a dear and trustworthy friend is supposed to pick you up at the dentist's office and drive you home. She's 30 minutes late. "What's going on?" you wonder. Your first thoughts turn to a traffic jam or an accident. You're worried.

However, if the person has caused you problems in the past, you may jump to a different conclusion. Say she's often been unreliable. Maybe she constantly criticizes you. Worse still, you're standing in the pouring rain while your head is pounding with a migraine.

Under adverse conditions people more readily make the fundamental attribution error. During accountability discussions, the fundamental attribution error is as predictable as gravity: "She's late because she's self-centered. She doesn't care about me. Just wait until she gets here!" The more tainted the history is and the more severe the consequences are, the more likely we are to assume the worst, become angry, and shoot from the hip.

Choosing Silence or Violence

Silence

Not everyone who tells an ugly story angrily leaps into a conversation ready to exact a pound of flesh, at least not immediately. For many people it takes a while to become upset, smug, or self-righteous. In fact, when we began studying accountability 25 years ago, we learned that the vast majority of the subjects we observed were inclined to walk away from violated promises, broken commitments, or bad behavior.

When we asked the subjects why they backed off, they explained that it was usually better not to deal with issues the first time they occurred. After all, many of those problems were anomalies. They weren't likely to be repeated, so why make a big deal and come off as a micromanager? There may be some truth to this, but as we suggested earlier, avoidance may be the real reason for the inaction; most of the research subjects in our study avoided taking action for fear of getting into a heated argument, which they assumed could lead to even more problems. Who could blame them for going to silence?

However, it's not as if choosing silence were a product of scientific inquiry. We back away from people because we conclude that they're selfish or rotten. Then we act on that conclusion as if it were the truth: "Who's going to approach these folks? They're selfish and rotten!" Therefore, we opt to stay silent.

No matter what the reason is, walking away from violated promises and broken commitments can be risky. When you see a violation but move to silence rather than deal with it, three bad things happen:

- First, you give tacit approval to the action. If you see an infraction and say nothing, the other person can easily conclude that you've given permission. *You* may feel that you've given permission, and then, realizing that you've given the action the green light, you find that it's harder to say something later.

- Second, others may think that you're playing favorites: "Hey, you never let me get away with that kind of stuff!"

- Third, each time the other person repeats the offense, in part because of your failure to deal with it, you see the new offense as evidence that your story about his or her motives was correct. You continue to tell yourself ugly stories, you fester and fuss, and it's only a matter of time until you blow.

Violence

Eventually, as problems gnaw at you, there comes a time when you can stand it no longer. You leap from silence to violence.

A person interrupts you in midsentence for the hundredth time, and you finally blow a gasket. Your assistant misses an important deadline for the hundredth time, and you come unglued. Of course, you may not become physically violent, but you do employ debating tactics, give people your famous stare, raise your voice, make threats, offer up ultimatums, insult the other person, use ugly labels, and otherwise rain violence on the conversation.

Surprised by your sudden and unexpected eruption, the other person thinks that you've lost all touch with reality. "Where did *that* come from?" he or she wonders. But alas, the other person knows the answer. You did it, he or she concludes, because you're stupid and evil. You've now helped *the other person* commit the fundamental attribution error about you, which feeds that person's silence or violence, and the cycle continues.

> Rare is the sudden and unexpected emotional explosion that wasn't preceded by a lengthy period of tortured silence.

Violence Is Costly

When you move from silence to violence, you no longer keep accountability discussions professional, under control, and on track to achieve a satisfactory ending. In fact, when you move to violence, the consequences can be nothing short of horrendous.

You Become Hypocritical, Abusive, and Clinically Stupid

Most of us have made a variety of vows through the years. Our parents punish us for something we believe is trivial, and we vow never to do the same thing to our children. We watch our boss lose her temper and swear that we'll never act so ghastly. We see a friend walk away from a moral stance and promise we'll never be that weak.

Unfortunately, those vows rarely keep us out of trouble. When we observe others, tell ourselves ugly stories, and then fall under the influence of adrenaline, we become the very people we swore we'd never be. Of course, nobody transmutes into a hypocritical cretin on purpose. Instead, stupidity creeps up on us. We tell ourselves an ugly story, become mentally incapacitated while under the effects of adrenaline, convince ourselves that we have the moral high ground, and move to either silence or violence while smugly proclaiming, "He *deserved* whatever I gave him."

Sometimes when we're really dumbed down by the effects of adrenaline, we make a truly absurd argument: "Sure I was tough on them, but you need to be tough with these people. They respond to abuse, not reason."

Actually, we don't have to be all that mentally incapacitated to make this argument. It's foisted on us almost every day, and with a straight face, no less. The fact that others need to be treated poorly to get them off their lazy back parts is sacred writ.

For instance, we praise coaches for their incredible records, and if they happen to be abusive, we actually attribute their success to their authoritarian and punitive style. Consider the Hollywood version of the 1980 U.S. national ice hockey team's miraculous gold medal victory. According to the movie, the coach abuses, insults, and manipulates the players because they need to be motivated and that is the way to do it. Apparently, the prospect of winning the Olympics isn't all that inspiring. He gets the players to hate him so that he can become the common enemy. That way they'll pull together as a team.

When the team wins the final match, audience members don't merely cheer the victory; they voice their approval of the coach's abusive methods. "What a guy!" people exclaim as they leave the theater. "What a leader!" Maybe we honor the abusive style of so many coaches and other public figures because their public actions lend credibility to our own private outbursts. Their tantrums, taunts, and tricks support our own claim that it was okay to emotionally attack our teenage son because "it was good for him."

Let's put this foolishness to bed. People don't *deserve* to be abused, physically or emotionally. It's *not good for them*. Yes, people should be held accountable. No one is questioning the need to act as responsible adults and expect others to do the same. But it is never good to abuse, insult, or threaten others. Friedrich Nietzsche once argued that what doesn't kill us makes us stronger. This little homily is often quoted. It's also often wrong. When it comes to emotions, abuse isn't a blessing; it's a curse.

When people gain success through abuse, they succeed in spite of their method, not because of it. For over five decades scholars have shown that abusive leadership styles don't succeed over the long haul, and over the short haul they're simply immoral. The greatest leaders, coaches, and parents we studied (and certainly all the positive deviants) never became abusive. And during those weak moments when they may have briefly stepped over the line, they never argued that others needed or deserved it.

Warning!

If you observe an infraction, tell yourself an ugly story, cut your brain power in half with a dose of adrenaline, and then do something abusive and stupid, don't say others deserved it or it was good for them. These words may sound logical when you can't see straight, or they may give you a warm glow when you're starting to question your aggressive actions, but the simple truth is there is no place for abuse of any kind at home, at work, or even on the playing field.

You Turn the Spotlight on Yourself

Imagine that you're on a flight across the Pacific. Seated nearby is a child who enjoys running up and down the aisle while screaming in a voice that could curdle milk. This continues for just long enough to turn the cabin passengers into a single seething entity with but one wish: to silence the child and return her to her seat. Suddenly, an older fellow next to you grabs the little girl by her frail arm and screams into her baby blues.

Guess what happens next. The passengers who once wanted to see the kid silenced now want to see the mean old man punished. In one swift motion the attention switches from the child to the abusive old guy. People are now sympathizing with the poor little girl. It takes only an instant to transfer goodwill.

The software development leaders learned this lesson the hard way. They might have approached the programmers with the angels on their side, but the instant they became abusive, they gave up the moral high ground. With each outburst, curse, and threat, they armed the original offenders with a good defense.

Of course, this doesn't mean that the original parties are off the hook, but it does mean that the leaders are now on the hook. Acting unprofessionally never earns you points. It takes the spotlight off the original offense and puts it on you at a time when you're on your worst behavior.

The Stories We Tell Help Us Justify Our Worst Behavior

Stories cause us to see the other person not as a human being but as a thing, and if not a thing, at least a villain. Stories exaggerate other people's legitimate weaknesses while turning a blind eye to our role. Stories help us see others as cretins and help justify our bad behaviors toward them, subtle or otherwise.

Here's the deal: You can't solve a problem with a villain. You can do that only with a human being. Before starting an accountability discussion, use everything in this chapter to help you come to see the other person as a *person*, perhaps a person doing really rotten things but a person nonetheless. This difference is everything. Accountability experts set a healthy climate by avoiding ugly stories.

How do you challenge your story, especially when it feels so right? What does it take to avoid making the fundamental attribution error, becoming angry, and then establishing a hostile climate?

THE SOLUTION: TELL THE REST OF THE STORY

Since the problem of coming up with ugly stories and suffering the consequences takes place within the confines of your own mind, that's where the solution lies as well. The positive deviants we study observe an infraction and then tell themselves a more complete and accurate story. Instead of asking, "What's the matter with that person?" they ask, "Why would a reasonable, rational, and decent person do that?"

By asking this "humanizing question," individuals who routinely master accountability discussions adopt a situational as well as a dispositional view of people. Instead of arguing that others are misbehaving only because of personal characteristics, influence masters look to the environment and ask, "What other sources of influence are acting on this person? What's causing this person to do that? Since this person is rational but appears to be acting either irrationally or irresponsibly, what am I missing?"

You can answer these questions only by developing a more complete view of humans and the circumstances that surround them than the traditional "What's wrong with them?" And if you do amplify your situational view, not only will you gain a deeper understanding of why people do what they do, but you'll eventually develop a diverse set of tools for managing accountability.

Consider The Six Sources of Influence™

To help expand our view of human behavior, we've organized the potential root causes of all behavior (including broken promises) into a model that contains six sources of influence. At the top of our model are two components of behavior selection. In order to take the required action, the person must be willing and able. Each of these components is affected by three sources of influence: self, others, and things.

Personal

Source 1. Personal Motivation

We already know the first source. It's the one that, considered alone, makes up the fundamental attribution error. People base their actions on their individual motivation or disposition. Does the action motivate? Does the person enjoy the action independent of how others think or feel? Does it bring pleasure or pain? That's the model we already have in our heads, and it's partially true. People do have personal motives. Human beings do take pleasure in certain activities, and it could even be true that they enjoy making us suffer. However, this model is also the source of influence that gets us in trouble when it's the only factor we consider.

Source 2. Personal Ability

We can double this simple model by adding individual ability. We now have two diagnostic questions: "Are others *motivated* to do what they promised?" and "Are they *able*?" (Does he or she have the skills or knowledge to do what's required?) By expanding the model from one to two sources, we acknowledge the fact that people not only must want to do what's required; they also need the mental and physical capacity to do it. For instance, maybe your company's customer-service agents aren't returning calls to hostile clients because they don't know how to defuse the hostility. Perhaps nurses aren't using protective gloves consistently because they can't put them on quickly enough.

With two options to choose from, we also have another story to tell ourselves. Rather than judging others who violate an expectation as unmotivated and therefore selfish and insensitive, we add the possibility that maybe they actually tried to live up to their promises but ran into a barrier.

Becoming Curious

Admitting that a problem might stem from several different sources will change our whole approach. We aren't certain, we aren't smug, we aren't angry, and we slow down. We're curious instead of boiling mad. We feel the need to gather more data rather than charge in "guns a-blazin'." We move from judge, jury, and executioner to curious participant.

Social

None of us works or lives in a vacuum. We make a promise, and more often than not we sincerely want to deliver on it. We may even have the talent to do so. But what happens when others enter the scene? Will coworkers, friends, and family members motivate us? Will they enable us? Social forces play such an important role in every aspect of our lives that any reasonable model of human behavior must include them.

Source 3. Social Motivation

From the way adults talk, you'd think peer pressure disappears a few weeks after the senior prom. We constantly warn our children against the insidious forces wielded by their friends. Yet rarely do we consider the fact that those forces aren't switched off in some secret ritual when we finish high school. Adult peer pressure may be less obvious than its teenage counterpart, but it's no less forceful.

For instance, what do you think will happen if the supervisor of the software testers walks up to one of them and says, "Hey, Chris, we're running behind schedule. Could you hurry things along?"

"What do you mean?" Chris asks.

"You know, maybe finesse, or even shorten, the final tests. The software seems to be running smoothly."

And with that simple request, the tests are dropped.

Is the other person being influenced by peers, the boss, customers, or family, or for that matter, by any other human being? Remember the work of Solomon Asch and Stanley Milgram? They created conditions in which social pressure drove people to change their opinions, lie, and even inflict pain on others. Should it surprise us that many of the ridiculous things both children and adults do are a result of simply wanting to be accepted by others? Healthcare professionals violate standards, scientists turn a blind eye to safety, accountants watch their peers break the law, and nobody says anything. Why? Because the presence of others who say nothing causes them to doubt their own beliefs, and their desire to be accepted taints their overall judgment. Social pressure is the mother of all stupidity.

Source 4. Social Ability

In addition to motivating you to do things, other people can enable or disable you. They're either a help or a hindrance. For you to complete your job, your coworkers have to provide you with help, information, tools, materials, and sometimes even permission. Unless you're working in a vacuum, if your coworkers don't do their part, you're dead in the water.

For example, what about the software engineers? What if their testing package failed? What if the person responsible for keeping the servers online went off to a technical seminar and didn't keep them up and running as long as needed? Who knows? Maybe that's why the software is giving final assembly fits. That is the whole point of this discussion. Who knows? We're going to have to gather data.

You're a Big Part of the Social Formula

Let's add one more piece to the social formula: you. You're a person too. You may be acting in ways that are contributing to the problem that is bothering you. You've got the eyeballs problem: you're on the wrong side of them if you want to notice the role you're playing. For example, a staff support person misses a deadline because she didn't like the way you made your initial request. She thought that when you rushed up to her, project in hand, the way you pushed for a commitment was too forceful, demanding, and insensitive to her needs. She didn't say anything, but she did find a way to put your request at the bottom of her priority list: "Sorry, I just never got around to it."

We encounter the same problem at home. You're at your wits' end because your husband is punishing and cold to your children (his stepchildren). You wonder why. Is he just selfish and impatient? Could it also be that you rarely show sympathy for his frustrations with them? Perhaps you are making him feel isolated and resentful about the challenges *he* faces, and that helps him feel more justified in behaving rudely to "your" children.

But that's not all. As a big part of others' "social influence," you can also affect their *ability* to meet your expectations. How about that time your son didn't complete his science project on time? You forgot to buy the ingredients for the volcano he was building on the way home from work. When that happened, of course, you realized that you were part of the problem. When you don't enable people, you're likely to notice your role, and others are certainly likely to say something to you if you let them down.

When your style or demeanor or methods cause resistance, others may purposefully clam up and not deliver, and you won't even know that you're the cause of the problem. You'll just hear a lot of excuses and get no honest feedback, particularly if you're in a position of authority. In this case, you need to turn your eyeballs inward and look for the whole story by asking yourself, "What, if anything, am I pretending not to notice about my role in the problem?"

You know people out there who do things that cause others to push back, resent them, reject their input, or drag their feet. Here's a news flash: sometimes you may be that person.

Structural

As you watch people going about their daily activities, you see that a great deal of what they do is affected by nonhuman factors. Much of what we do is a function of the structural world around us. This isn't always obvious to the untrained eye. In fact, many of us are fairly insensitive to the effects of our *own* surroundings, let alone the surroundings of others.

For example, you're trying to lose weight and don't realize that the cash or credit cards you're carrying enable you to set aside the lunch you packed and buy a high-calorie restaurant meal. You're hungry (personal motive), your friends ask you to lunch (social motive), and the credit card you're carrying (structural motive) puts you over the top. You also don't see the distance to the fridge as a factor or the fact that you fill it with unhealthy foods as a force. Of course, all are having an impact.

Human beings don't intuitively turn to the environment, organizational forces, institutional factors, and other *things* when they look at what's causing behavior. We often miss the impact that equipment, materials, work layout, or temperature is having on behavior. We've also been known to miss the way goals, roles, rules, information, technology, and other *things* motivate and enable.

Source 5. Structural Motivation

How do things motivate us? That's simple enough. Money (and what it can get us) motivates people; that we know. Guess what happens when money is aimed at the wrong targets? For instance, managers are rewarded for keeping costs down, and hourly employees are rewarded for working overtime. They're constantly arguing with each other. Quality specialists earn bonuses for checking material, and production employees earn bonuses for shipping it. They too seem to have trouble getting along. Maybe a team-building exercise will reduce the tension. Perhaps conflict-resolution training will help. Yeah, right.

When they explore underlying causes, experienced leaders quickly turn to the formal reward system and look at the impact that money, promotions, job assignments, benefits, bonuses, and all the other organizational rewards are having on behavior. It is sheer folly to reward A while hoping for B. Savvy leaders and effective parents get this.

Here's how this concept applies to a community example. One of the greatest challenges in influencing "at-risk" youth in inner-city areas is that the models of successful careers that they see often involve the sale of illegal drugs. It isn't just the influence of *others* that lures them into illicit trade; it's *financial*. Until they see clear alternative pathways to financial well-being, thousands of young men and women will be lost to this social cancer.

Frustrated couples are no less strongly affected by this powerful source of influence. The foundations of thousands of marriages continue to erode as one or both spouses give their hearts to careers that promise increased status or rich rewards to those who pay the price.

Source 6. Structural Ability

When it comes to ability, *things* can often provide either a bridge or a barrier. For example, imagine you're trying to get the people in marketing to meet more regularly with the people in production. They currently avoid each other because they don't get along. You've aligned their goals and rewards, but marketers still call production folks "thugs" and production specialists call marketers "slicks." You believe that if you can get them in the same room once in a while, many of their problems will go away. But how? What will it take to get them to meet more often and eventually collaborate?

First you write an inspiring memo. Nothing happens. Then you add "interdepartmental collaboration" to the company's performance-review form. Nada. Next comes a speech, then veiled threats, and finally you create an award program that honors the "Collaborator of the Month." You tell the various division heads to nominate an employee for the award, and they argue endlessly about who should win.

Now you decide to do some out-of-the-box thinking, only this time it's out-of-the-cashbox thinking. The heck with rewards; it's time to turn to other *things*. Could you do something to the physical aspects of the organization that would allow people to interact more easily and more often?

Yes, you could. In fact, if you want to get the two groups to meet more often, think proximity. When it comes to the frequency of human interaction, proximity (the distance between people) is the single best predictor. Individuals who are located close to one another bump into each other and talk.

When it comes to work, people who share a break room or resource pool tend to bump into each other as well. Move the marketing offices closer to the work floor, throw in a common area, and the two groups may warm to each other. Proximity or the lack thereof has an invisible but powerful effect on behavior.

The following are a few other structural forces that can affect ability.

Gadgets

Gadgets can have a more profound impact on behavior than most people imagine. For example:

- Cooks and waitresses used to fight tooth and nail over what had been ordered and whose orders got filled first until a researcher invented the metal wheel that controls and organizes orders. With the advent of the wheel, waitresses stopped shouting commands at cooks, and cooks stopped getting angry and purposefully fouling up the orders.

- A mother was constantly punishing her young son for not coming home before dark. The boy didn't know when the end of "before dark" was, would wait until it was actually dark, and got in trouble—until his neighbor gave him a watch and his mother gave him a specific time to be home.

- A father turned the hot water off at the source so that his wife and daughters wouldn't take so long in the shower. They resented his actions. One day Mom put an egg timer in the shower, and the problem went away.

- One family determined that its microwave had put distance between the parents and their children. Was this a lame excuse? Not when one realizes that their first microwave eliminated the one time the whole family came together: the evening meal. With their fancy new zapper, the children were able to make what they wanted when they wanted. Without realizing it, the family members lost a key force and began to pull in separate directions. The point is not that gadgets are bad but that they can have a more significant impact on human behavior than people might imagine.

Data

A financial services company couldn't get people to help cut costs until it published both cost data and financial records. With the same goal in mind, factories now prominently display the cost of each part. In a large intercity hospital, the health-care professionals regularly chose to use rubber gloves ($30 a pair) instead of less comfortable latex gloves ($3 a pair), even for short procedures. After endless memos encouraging people to save money, administrators posted the cost of the gloves in prominent locations, and glove expenses dropped overnight.

One wise parent tired of the endless requests of his teenage daughter for everything from designer tennis shoes to a luxury sports car. One evening it struck him that an ounce of information might be worth a pound of accountability discussions. He openly shared *everything* about the family finances. Eventually his daughter—and we're not making this up—asked if she should get a night job to help out.

Completing the Story

When you encounter people who aren't living up to a commitment, it's easy to wonder what were they thinking. Left to our natural proclivities, we tell a simple yet ugly story that casts others as selfish or thoughtless. We mature a little bit every time we expand the story to include a person's ability. Maybe others don't know how to do what they've promised to do. We also cut off our anger at its source. Not knowing for certain what's happening, we have to replace anger with curiosity. This puts us in a far better position to discuss an infraction as a scientist, not a vigilante.

Throw in the influence of *others,* and the story starts to reflect the complexity of what's really going on. The fact that social forces are likely to be a huge part of any infraction doesn't escape a savvy problem solver. Only a fool purposely pits people against their desire to belong, feel respected, and be included with their friends and colleagues. Understanding the influence of others is a prerequisite to effective accountability.

Finally, if we really want to step into the ranks of those who master accountability, we need to consider the structural factors, or *things,* surrounding a violated promise. This isn't intuitive. In fact, rare is the parent or leader who looks at either the reward structure or other environmental factors when trying to diagnose the root cause of a behavior. Learn how to do this, and you'll be in a class of your own.

Use the Six Sources of Influence

Combined, these six distinct and powerful sources make up the Six-Source Model, a diagnostic and influence tool that was illustrated earlier in this chapter.

How About Our Software-Testing Friends?

What actually caused the software problem during final assembly? Several of the forces contained in our model played a role:

- A supervisor had been sent to the scene, where she learned that the programmers were unfamiliar with the latest version of the testing software (personal ability).

- The supervisor had offered to obtain a tutorial, but the material was located across town at headquarters (structural ability). The team leader said he'd get it, but didn't (social ability).

- The team leader never received the material because he was stopped in the hallway, where he was told to prepare for a "walk-by" from a big boss from headquarters (social motive).

Did the code writers skip the testing because they didn't like doing it? That could have been the case, but it wasn't. Consequently, if the managers had punished the operators for not being motivated, it wouldn't have remedied any of the underlying causes and most certainly would have caused resentment.

One Final Comment

The best leaders and parents aren't lax with accountability, nor do they let themselves stew in a stupor of self-loathing. If the other person does turn out to be at fault, those who are masters of accountability step up to and handle the failed promise. In fact, we'll explore how to do exactly that in later chapters.

For now we're merely trying to work on our first thought, our first look into a possible infraction, and the tone that follows. We're learning to fight our natural tendency to assume the worst of others and replace it with genuine curiosity to ensure that our first words and deeds create a healthy climate for ourselves and others. When we *tell the rest of the story*, we do exactly that.

CHAPTER SUMMARY

Master My Stories

Now we've selected a violated expectation and thought about the surrounding circumstances in a way that puts us in the best state of mind. In short, we've learned how to master our stories by seeking out all the possible sources of influences that affect the problem.

- *Master my stories.* The second step in the model also takes place before you actually speak. As you approach an accountability discussion, take care you don't establish a horrible climate by charging in half-informed and half-cocked. To avoid this costly mistake, work on your own thoughts, feelings, and stories before you utter a word

- *Tell the rest of the story.* Ask why a reasonable, rational, and decent person would do what you've just seen as well as if you yourself are playing a role in the problem.

- *Look at all six sources of influence.* Examine personal, social, and structural sources—all either motivate or enable others to keep their commitment.

- *Expand motive to include the influence of others.* Do others praise and support the desired behavior, or do they provide pressure against it? Is the reward system aligned? If people do what's required, will they receive a reward or punishment?

- *Finally, add ability.* Can others do what's required? Does the requisite task play to their strength or weakness? Are people around them a help or a hindrance? Do the things around them provide a bridge or a barrier?

What's Next?

Now that we're fully prepared, it's time to open our mouths and talk about the violated promise. How do we first talk about the infraction we've observed? What should be the first words out of our mouths? Let's take a look.

Part Two

Create Safety

What to Do During an Accountability Crucial Conversation

When you create enough safety, you can talk to almost anyone about almost anything. As those who are masters of accountability move from thinking to talking, here's how they create safety:

- They begin well. They know how to describe a performance gap in a way that makes it safe for others to talk about with them (Chapter 3, "Describe the Gap").

- They know how to help others prioritize competing demands, and they know how to discipline when necessary (Chapter 4, "Make It Motivating").

- They also know how to help others deal with ability barriers by jointly exploring solutions. They *help* others comply by making compliance easier. They understand the underlying principles of empowerment (Chapter 5, "Make It Easy").

- Finally, they also know how to deal with unexpected problems or emotions that may come up during an accountability discussion (Chapter 6, "Stay Focused and Flexible").

3

Describe the Gap
How to Start an Accountability Crucial Conversation

I'M SORRY, BUT MY OSMOSIS IS BROKEN

You've picked out a broken commitment, decided to say something, and considered the six possible sources of influence behind it; now you are about to say something. Before you do that, let's be clear. Almost nobody should be harboring the illusion that he or she has been groomed to solve touchy and complicated accountability challenges. Almost nobody has.

Here's a typical supervisory training regime. A hardworking and competent employee is tapped on the shoulder on Friday afternoon ("Congratulations, you won the supervisory lottery!") and promoted to a job that starts Monday morning. Any questions? And it's not as if most employees have actually watched the way a leader deals with touchy issues or failed promises. That kind of thing happens behind closed doors.

Of course, business schools, the breeding ground for managers and vice presidents, rarely teach anything about face-to-face leadership. Most business school courses are about management and entrepreneurship, not leadership. Occasionally classes cover the way leaders should *think* but almost never what they should *do.* The curriculum certainly doesn't cover accountability discussions. Professors and students routinely encounter violated expectations, but almost nobody teaches how to handle them.

We don't even want to think about the preparation the average parent receives. Heaven forbid that most of us should imitate the social skills of our own adult role models: "Thanks, Mom. I was afraid I was going to miss out on how to paralyze people with guilt, but you've taken time every single day to pass on an important lesson or two."

Here's the $64,000 question: How are people supposed to have picked up the ability to hold a simple goal-setting session, let alone tap-dance through a thorny accountability discussion? Through osmosis?

If your human interaction training has been as sketchy as everyone else's, welcome to the club and be sure to pay close attention. We're about to share the best practices of the positive deviants who know how to walk up to someone and hold an effective accountability discussion.

EXACTLY WHAT ARE WE TALKING ABOUT?

Before we dare to open our mouths, let's make sure we're thinking about the same topic. Exactly what is the topic of our upcoming conversation?

We're stepping up to a:

violated expectation
a gap: a difference between what you expected and what actually happened. Gaps are typically thought of as:

Violated Promises, Broken Commitments, and Bad Behaviors

As far as this book is concerned, when we say "gap," we mean *serious, consequential, and complex deviations*, something that might be hard or even risky to discuss. Anybody can sidle up to a cheerful and eager employee and discuss a minor infraction. You don't need a book to take that kind of trivial action.

Instead, as we suggested earlier, we'll be exploring challenges such as the following: What's the best way to confront your boss for micromanaging you? How do you talk to a friend about backbiting? How do you tell a doctor she's not doing her job? What does it take to discipline a violent employee? We call the topic of this book *crucial* accountability because the stakes are high. Handle things poorly, and you could lose a job, a friend, or a limb.

Know What Not to Do

We'll start our exploration of ways to initiate an accountability discussion by sharing what we've learned not only from studying our positive deviants but also from observing people who had the guts to step up to a problem but then quickly failed. After all, knowing what *not* to do is half the battle.

Don't Play Games

The first technique for starting an accountability discussion is the child of good intentions married to bad logic. It's called sandwiching. You honestly believe that you have two equally poor options (and no other choices). You can stay quiet and keep the peace, or you can be honest and hurt someone's feelings. So you use sandwiching in an earnest effort to be both nice and honest. To soften the violent blow, you first say something complimentary, next you bring up the problem, and then you close with something complimentary again. Here is an example.

> *"Hey, Bob, good-looking briefcase. By the way, do you know anything about the 10 grand missing from our retirement fund? Love the haircut."*

A close cousin to this circuitous technique takes the form of a surprise attack. A leader starts a conversation in a chatty tone, makes pleasant small talk, and then suddenly moves in for the kill.

The most unpleasant of these backhanded approaches is unadulterated entrapment—where one person lures the other into denying a problem, only to punish him or her for lying. It sounds something like this:

> *"How were things at school today?"*
> *"Fine. Same old stuff."*
> *"Fine? The principal called and said you started a food fight in the cafeteria. Is that supposed to be fine?"*

Most people despise these indirect techniques. They're dishonest, manipulative, and insulting. They're also quite common.

Don't Play Charades

Rather than come right out and talk about a missed commitment, many people rely on nonverbal hints and subtle innuendo. They figure that's faster and safer than actually talking about a problem. Some deal almost exclusively in hints. For instance, to make their point, they frown, smirk, or look concerned. When somebody's late, they glance at their watches. This vague approach is fraught with risk. People may get the message, but what if they misinterpret the nonverbal hints? Besides, how are you supposed to document your actions?

> *"February 10, 2 p.m. Raised my right eyebrow three centimeters. Employee nodded knowingly and started back to work."*

Don't Pass the Buck

Another bad way to begin an accountability discussion is rooted in the erroneous belief that you can play the role of good cop if only you can find a way to transform the person's boss into the bad cop. Parents play the same game by bad-mouthing or blaming their mates. By being the "pleasant one," they believe, they're more likely to stay on civil terms with their direct reports or children. Here's the kind of stunt they pull:

> *"I know you don't want to work late, but the big guy says that if you don't, we'll write you up. If I had my way, we'd all go home early for the holiday weekend."*

This strategy is disloyal, dishonest, and ineffective. Anyone who wasn't raised by wolves can see through it. Nothing undermines your authority more than blaming someone else for requesting what you would be asking for if you had any guts. If you repeat this mistake, it won't be long before you're seen as irrelevant—merely a messenger, and a cowardly one at that.

Don't Play "Read My Mind"

If you scour the bookstores, eventually you may stumble across a few accountability texts that make the following suggestion: "Since people benefit from learning on their own, don't come right out and tell them about the actual infraction that has you concerned. Instead, allow room for 'self-discovery.'" Make the guilty person guess what's on your mind. Here's what this can look like:

> *"Well, Carmen, why do you think I called you in so bright and early this morning?"*
> *"I don't know. Is it because I crashed the company car?"*
> *"Nope."*
> *"Hmmm, was it because I sabotaged the phone system?"*
> *"Wrong again."*
> *"Is it because . . ."*

This tactic is as irritating as it is ineffective. Despite good intentions, asking others to read your mind typically comes off as patronizing or manipulative.

Learn from Positive Deviants

For every person we watched play games and fail, we were privileged to observe a skilled parent, supervisor, or manager in action. These people were something to behold. When we first chose to tag along after top performers, we were surprised to see how similar their styles were, independent of the industry. We expected to find muted, even sensitive, behavior in high-tech firms, universities, and banks, but we anticipated something quite different in mines, foundries, and factories. We were wrong. Melissa, one of the effective frontline supervisors in the manufacturing facility that had lost most elements of accountability, found a way to be both honest *and* respectful and quickly became the most effective leader in the facility.

To be honest, when we first watched Melissa, we thought that her style was—how does one say it?—gender specific. So we asked if we could watch the other positive deviant—one of the plant's rather large and scary male supervisors, but one who relied on interpersonal skills rather than threats, abuse, and intimidation.

True to what we had learned about Melissa, Buford (the first hard-hat accountability expert we trailed) seemed far more like Mr. Rogers than Mr. T. Despite the fact that the facility appeared to have been prefabricated in hell, Buford's style and demeanor could have fit easily into a white-collar boardroom. He acted far more like a schoolteacher than like the abusive leaders who surrounded him.

When we asked the plant manager why he thought Melissa and Buford were the best of the best, he repeated something we learned earlier. "It's easy to find a leader who creates warm and lasting relationships but who struggles to get things done. It's not much harder to find a no-nonsense, hard-hitting leader whom you might send in to put out a fire but who creates hard feelings. Consequently, when you find someone who can manage both people and production, you've got a real gem."

How did these two skilled professionals solve problems while building relationships? How did they start an accountability discussion? We're not sure how they came to have the same understanding, but it didn't take us long to realize that the skilled leaders and parents we eventually studied had somehow managed to stumble onto the same exquisitely simple yet important principles.

DESCRIBE THE GAP

To ensure that you set the right tone during the first few seconds of any accounting, don't shoot from the hip. Don't charge into a situation, kick rears, take names, and let the chips fall where they may. Instead, carefully describe the gap. Here's how:

- Start with safety.
- Share your path.
- End with a question.

Start with Safety

When another person has let you down, start the conversation by simply describing the gap between what was expected and what was observed: "You said you were going to have your room cleaned before dinner. It's nine o'clock, and it's still not done."

Don't play games; merely describe the gap. Describing what was expected versus what was observed is clear and simple, and it helps you get off on the right foot.

For the most part, this is how you'll begin an accountability discussion. However, if you have reason to believe that the other person will feel threatened or intimidated or insulted by the mere mention of the violated promise, you'll need to take steps to ensure that he or she feels safe—no matter the infraction.

As we noted earlier, we watched skilled individuals talk about incompetence, mistrust, and even embezzling, and the conversations, though not always pleasant, ended successfully. Then we watched less skilled individuals raise something as trivial as arriving five minutes late to a meeting, and the conversation degenerated into a shouting match.

As we tried to understand these apparent contradictions, we finally realized what was happening.

The Big Surprise

At the foundation of every successful accountability discussion lies safety. When others feel unsafe, you can't talk about anything. But if you can create safety, you can talk with almost anyone about almost anything—even about failed promises.

Of course, the more controversial and touchy the issue is, the more challenging the conversation will be. Nevertheless, if you maintain a safe climate, others will hear and consider what you're saying. They may not like it, but they'll be able to absorb it. Make it safe for people, and they won't need to go to silence or violence.

Let's take a look at what it takes to create and maintain a safe climate, beyond simply describing the gap. Let's examine how to open our mouths and talk about a violated expectation when we're suspicious that the other person might become defensive or upset.

Watch for Signs That Safety Is at Risk

Let's quickly review the basics of safety and then move to the task of making it safe, even when you're dealing with a mammoth broken promise.

People feel unsafe when they believe one of two things:

1. You don't respect them as human beings (you lack Mutual Respect).

2. You don't care about their goals (you lack Mutual Purpose).

When others know that you value them as a person and care about their interests, they will give you an amazing amount of leeway. They'll let you say almost anything. That's why your four-year-old granddaughter can tell you you're "fat" without offending you. You know that she loves and respects you and that her motives are pure. This, after all, is an innocent child. However, if *what* you say or *how* you say it causes others to conclude that you don't respect them or that you have selfish and perverse motives, nothing you say will work. Here's why.

As you talk to others about a gap in performance, a warning flag goes up in their minds. After all, this is a problem discussion. They immediately want to know one thing: Are they in trouble? Their boss, parent, loved one, or friend is bringing up an infraction, not inviting them to lunch. Are bad things going to happen? People assess their risk on the basis of two factors. Are bad things currently happening to them? Are bad things about to happen to them?

Mutual Respect

As you first describe the gap, if your tone of voice, facial expression, or words show disrespect, bad things are *currently* happening to the other person. You're not respecting that person. You're speaking in an uncivil tone. Your manner is discourteous. Your delivery is contemptuous. In short, you've held court in your head and found that person guilty, or so it feels to him or her.

Of course, this lack of respect is typically communicated subtly, not overtly. Sometimes it only takes a raised eyebrow. (On other occasions the word *moron* finds its way into the conversation.) In any case, the other person believes that you think he or she is incompetent, lazy, or worse. You have signaled that this conversation is going to end badly. After all, it's certainly starting that way. It's only natural that when others feel disrespected, they feel unsafe and resort to either silence or violence.

Mutual Purpose

Let's look at safety problems that extend beyond the moment. If it becomes clear to others that your purpose is at odds with theirs, they're likely to conclude that something bad is about to happen to them. You're going to deal with an infraction, and if they're harmed in the process, so be it. Your goal is to get what you want, and you aren't even thinking about their goal. This doesn't bode well for them. Even if you start the conversation respectfully, it's only natural that if others feel that you are at cross-purposes, they'll resort to silence or violence. They have to watch out for their interests.

> At the very first sign of fear, you have to diagnose. Are others feeling disrespected? Or do they believe you're at cross-purposes? Or both? Then you have to find a way to let others know that you respect them and that you're not going to trample all over their wishes.

This can be hard to remember in the face of holding someone accountable. We typically care so much about the content of a conversation that we don't think to watch for fear and restore safety. Nevertheless, it's the only solution. We have to watch for signs that people are worried, stop saying what we're saying, diagnose why people are fearful, step out of the original conversation, and then restore Mutual Respect, Mutual Purpose, or both. Here's how to do that.

Maintain Mutual Respect

You're about to suggest that the other person has violated an expectation, and this could easily imply that he or she was not motivated, was not able, or both; and nobody likes to be told that. And if the infraction is huge, say, infidelity or lying, isn't the other person going to assume that you don't respect him or her—almost by definition? What can you do to ensure that the other person doesn't feel disrespected even though you're about to talk about a high-stakes performance gap?

Remember to Tell the Rest of the Story

Obviously, everything we've talked about so far helps create safety. First, we avoid making others feel disrespected by not disrespecting them. If we see a problem, tell ourselves an ugly story, and then charge in with an accusation, the other person is going to feel disrespected. Even if we find others guilty in our heads and do our best to hide it, the verdict will show on our faces.

Show others respect by giving them the benefit of the doubt. Tell the rest of the story. Think of other people as rational, reasonable, and decent. This attitude eventually affects our demeanor, choice of words, and delivery and helps make the conversation safe for others. They can tell that even though we've spotted a potential problem, we're speaking out of a position of respect.

Use Contrasting to Restore Mutual Respect

Sometimes thinking good thoughts is not enough. We're pleasant as we begin to talk about a failed promise, but the other person hears the mention of a problem and immediately assumes that we do not respect him or her. A problem is a bad thing, the other person is connected to the problem, and therefore we must think he or she is bad. Despite our best efforts, others feel unsafe and go to silence or violence, and we haven't even made it all the way through our first sentence.

Let's add a skill to help us with our very first sentence. We'll use it as a preemptive tool for stopping disrespect in its tracks. It's called *Contrasting*. It's the killer of the fundamental attribution error. Here's how it works.

Before you start the conversation, anticipate how others might assume the worst. How might they feel disrespected? For instance, if you bring up a quality problem, the other person may believe that you think he or she is unskilled in general. If you address poor effort on a specific project, the other person may conclude that you believe he or she isn't motivated or can't be trusted, or perhaps you don't like him or her or are about to take disciplinary action, and so on. You've noticed a problem, and the other person prepares for the worst before you can finish your thought.

To deal with these predictable misinterpretations, use Contrasting. First, imagine what others might erroneously conclude. Second, immediately explain that this is what you don't mean. Third, as a Contrasting point, explain what you do mean. The important part is the "don't" portion. It addresses misunderstandings that could put safety at risk. Once safety is protected or reestablished, the "do" part of the statement clarifies your real meaning or intent. Here's what Contrasting sounds like when it is used up front to avoid feelings of disrespect:

> *"I don't want you to think I'm unhappy with how we work together. Overall I'm very satisfied. I just want to talk about how we make decisions together."*
>
> *"I'm not saying that it was wrong of you to disagree with me in the meeting. We need to hear everyone's view if we want to make the best choice. It's just that I think the team heard your tone and words as attacking."*
>
> *"I know you tried your best to improve your grades. I'm satisfied with your effort. Please don't hear me as being less*

than proud of your progress. I'd just like to share a few study ideas that might help you maintain your grades more easily."

Contrasting plays a huge role in initially describing broken promises. The bigger the problem is, the more likely it is that the other person is going to feel disrespected. Consequently, many discussions of broken promises and bad behavior start with a preventive Contrasting statement. In fact, this is the skill that people are typically looking for when they pick up a book that deals with missed expectations, because it answers the question "How do I get the conversation started?"

> If you suspect that the other person is going to feel offended or defensive, prepare the ground by explaining what you don't and do mean.

Of course, you can also use Contrasting in the middle of a conversation when you suddenly become aware that the other person is feeling disrespected. You didn't anticipate the reaction, but sure enough, he or she has found a way to feel disrespected:

"I'm sorry; I didn't mean to imply that you were doing it on purpose. I believe you were unaware of the impact you were having. That's why I wanted to bring it up in the first place."

Establish Mutual Purpose

When an accountability discussion turns ugly, with greater intensity and speed than you ever imagined it could, it's usually because others misunderstand not your *content* but your *intent*. You're speaking respectfully. That part you got right. You merely want to deal with the performance gap in a way that keeps the relationship on solid footing. Unfortunately, the people you're talking to think differently. They believe that the only reason you're bringing up the infraction is that you're out to humiliate them, make them do something they don't want to do, overthrow their authority, or otherwise cause them pain and sorrow. They believe that bad things are *about to happen* to them. Once again, mental math comes into play.

Of course, once others allow vicious stories about your intent to romp freely inside their brains, they become angry, defensive, and emotionally charged. Blood rushes to their arms and legs so that they can be better equipped for the fight-or-flight reaction their bodies have been genetically designed for.

Within seconds they're on their worst brain-starved behavior. Once this chemical transformation happens, there's a good chance you'll never get back on track. Anything you say carries with it the stench of evil intentions. And of course, since *they* are now dumbed down by adrenaline, their logical processes take a vacation, and nothing you say really matters.

You can't let this happen. If you think others are likely to harbor bad thoughts about your intentions before you've even said a word, take a second preventive measure: establish Mutual Purpose.

> Build common ground before you even mention a problem. Let others know that your intentions are pure—that your goal is to solve a performance gap and make things better for both of you. Start with what's important to you and them—not just you. Establish Mutual Purpose.

Here's an example:

> *"If it's okay with you, I'd like to spend a couple of minutes talking about how we made that last decision. My goal is to come up with a method we're both comfortable with."*
>
> *"I'd like to give you some feedback that I think would help you be more productive with your meetings.* [Add Contrasting.] *I don't think this is a huge problem, but I do think that if you were to make a couple of small changes, things would run a lot more smoothly."*

Note: If your sole purpose is to make your life better while possibly making the other person's life worse, who can blame others for becoming defensive? If there is a short-term cost associated with the change you're calling for (and there usually is), think about how everyone will benefit over the long haul and then establish Mutual Purpose. For example:

> *"I'm concerned about a problem that is affecting all of us. If we don't find a way to increase our output, we'll cease to be competitive. Our customer is already research-ing alternative sources, and we're at risk of being shut down. [Add Contrasting.] I don't want to come up with a plan that is physically or mentally stressing, because we'll have to live with it for years to come. I just want to develop a plan that leads to a more consistent and predict-able effort."*

Ask for Permission

If the gap you're about to address is traditionally off limits, par-ticularly sensitive, or something a person in your position doesn't normally discuss, ask for permission to discuss it. Be gracious. Don't plunge into a delicate topic without first seeking permis-sion. Asking permission is a powerful sign of respect and is par-ticularly helpful if you're speaking from a position of authority. It also helps allay people's suspicion that your intentions toward them are malicious.

Speak in Private

This tip is both obvious and easy: always hold accountability discussions in private. No matter where you may encounter a gap, retire to your office or another secluded setting where you can talk one-on-one. Never conduct public performance reviews. Never discipline your children in front of their friends. Never confront your spouse in the middle of a dinner party. Never talk about friends, loved ones, direct reports, or bosses at the water cooler. Speak in private, one-to-one and face-to-face. Avoid the following common violations of this principle.

Inappropriate Humor

Don't violate privacy by masking a public performance review with thoughtless humor, as in this example: "Well, look who just arrived. Forget how to find the meeting room, did you?"

For many people this is a hard habit to break. It takes years to learn how to craft the perfect public punitive remark: veiled enough to deny, clever enough to get a laugh, and pointed enough to be nasty. Nevertheless, drop the cutting sarcasm.

A Group Attack

Don't deal with individual infractions in meetings or public gatherings by chastising the entire group. This cowardly tactic fails doubly. First, the guilty parties may miss the fact that they're the target of your comments. Second, the innocent people resent the fact that they're being thrown in with the guilty. Once again, accountability should be done in private, one-on-one.

Combining Safety Skills

Let's see how these safety skills can be combined to help form the first few phrases in an accountability discussion, particularly if the topic is touchy or the person you're dealing with is in a position of power. How, for example, could you start with safety when conversing with a defensive boss?

Watching Wally

Let's watch Wally, a skilled communicator, as he deals with a defensive chief executive officer who is about to torpedo a project that Wally has invested a year in launching. This text is taken from an actual interaction between a manager and the CEO of his company.

CEO: You mean to say that we're going to spend three months gathering data? What a crock! I don't want to gather more data; I want to do something.

Wally recognizes the boss's outbreak for what it is. It is not a sign that the issue is off limits. He realizes that the boss is getting hot under the collar because safety is at risk. The boss needs to know that Wally cares about his interests and respects his position, so that's exactly what Wally communicates.

WALLY: Let me be clear on something. I don't want to waste any time or resources on something that adds no value. If gathering data is a waste, I will whack it from the plan in a heartbeat. I understand that you are facing a tough deadline, and at the end of this discussion I will do what you think needs to be done.

Now, with safety restored, Wally steps back into the issue at hand.

WALLY: With that said, I think there will be some negative consequences if we don't gather more data. I'll be happy to describe them, and then we can decide how to proceed.

At this point the CEO feels safe about where the conversation is going and asks to hear Wally's concerns. At the conclusion the CEO agrees that data gathering is critical and willingly supports the next steps.

Share Your Path

Let's look at the second step in describing a performance gap. We started with safety and will be doing our best to watch for fear throughout the discussion. When called for, we may start with a preemptive Contrasting statement or describe our common ground. Once the other person feels safe, it's now time to describe the gap.

Common Mistakes

To get us started on the actual words we'll choose, we'll begin with one of our favorite research subjects, Bruno. He was among the first leaders the authors watched on the job. We selected Bruno not because he was great but because he consistently demonstrated (note the root of the word: *demon*) all that is bad and wrong. He taught us what *not* to do.

Don't Keep Others in the Dark

It's 10 minutes into the workday, and the authors are roaming the floor with Bruno as he meanders through a nest of cubicles teeming with technicians.

"Watch this," Bruno fiendishly giggles as he approaches one of his direct reports. Bruno then circles the fellow like a vulture, shakes his head in disgust, mutters under his breath, and then flutters away.

The technician is clearly alarmed.

"Keep 'em on their toes," Bruno declares. "That's my motto." True to his word, for four straight hours Bruno explains nothing in clear terms. He constantly prods people with ambiguous expressions such as "shape up," "fix that," "that could kill someone," and the ever-popular "get a better attitude."

Nobody understood this guy. His tactics were as manipulative as they were ineffective. Strangely enough, Bruno was purposely vague. He used ambiguity as a torture device. But that was Bruno. Most people don't try to be vague; they're merely inarticulate. Whatever the root cause, lack of clarity is accountability's worst enemy. People can't fix a gap if they don't know the specific details of the infraction.

Back to the Model

To be crystal clear about the details we want to discuss, let's return to the Path to Action model. It explains how humans move from observation to action.

Remember this diagram, which was first introduced in Chapter 2? The other person acts, you see something, you tell yourself a story about the other person's motive, you feel, and then you act. Here's the question: What details should you talk about? What part of the path should you share: the action, your conclusion, or your feeling? How do you share your path?

No Harsh Conclusions, Please

When we step up to an accountability discussion, we're inclined to lead with judgments or stories. After all, our view of others' intent often has us all riled up. As far as we're concerned, their bad intent *is* the problem. Unfortunately, when we lead with our judgments, we get off on the wrong foot. It sounds something like this:

- "I can't believe that you purposely made fun of me in that meeting!"

- "You don't care about our family one tiny bit. Must you work every waking hour?"

- "You show no confidence. No wonder nobody trusts your opinion."

When we share our harsh stories, others now know what we have *concluded*, but they don't know what they have done. They can only guess at what we're talking about. This strategy can be unclear, inaccurate, and costly.

Start with Facts

As a general rule, when you are sharing your path, it's best to start with the facts: what you saw and heard. Don't lead with your stories. If you do, people are likely to become defensive. Instead, describe what the person did.

- *Stay external.* Describe what's happening outside your head ("You cut the person off in midsentence") as opposed to what's happening inside your head ("You're rude").

- *Explain what, not why.* Facts tell us what's going on ("You spoke so quietly, it was hard to hear"). Conclusions tell us why we think it's going on ("You're afraid").

- *Gather facts.* If others complain to you about their friends and coworkers, they're likely to tell stories and leave out the facts: "He's arrogant." "She's unreliable." "Their team is selfish." When this happens, probe for details. Ask them to share what they actually heard and saw.

Even when it comes to our own thinking, it's often difficult to remember the original facts. Most of us have an experience ("You spoke nonstop about yourself and didn't ask me a single question"), tell a story ("You're egotistical"), generate a feeling ("I don't like being around you"), and then forget the original experience. In some cases we may not even be aware of the other person's subtle action that led to the feeling. Thus, we end up walking around with feelings and stories but are incapable of holding a successful accountability discussion because we lack the facts required to help others understand what we're thinking.

Gathering the Facts Is the Homework Required for Holding an Accountability Discussion

Here's the bottom line. Every time you share a vague and possibly inflammatory story instead of a fact, you're betting that the other person won't become defensive and can translate what you're thinking into what he or she did. That's a bad bet. Share the facts. Describe the observable details of what's happening. Cut out the guesswork.

Tentatively Share Your Story

As we suggested earlier, sometimes a person's behavior can be moderately annoying, and maybe that individual has even broken a promise, but what really has you distressed is the fact that you believe that his or her *intent* is less than noble. You're trying not to make the fundamental attribution error, but facts are starting to pile up, and it's hard to keep assuming the best. Keeping an open mind is one thing; being naive is another.

Remember the realtor who was upset at an employee not just because she was routinely late but because the realtor figured she was taking advantage of their friendship? We suggested that this was the right problem to discuss or at least the correct starting point. But how do you merely discuss the facts when it's your story you want to talk about?

You don't. You share your story as well. Of course, you don't start there, but you don't walk away from your story either. Start with the facts because they're the least emotional and controversial element of the conversation and then tentatively share your story or conclusion. Make sure your language is free of absolutes. Trade "You said" for "I thought we agreed." Swap "It's clear" for "I was wondering if." Here's what this might sound like:

"Martha, I was wondering if we could talk about something that has me bothered. I'm not sure I'm correct in my thinking, so I thought I'd better check with you."

"Sure, what's the deal?"

"I've talked to you four different times about coming into work between 20 and 30 minutes late, and I'm beginning. . . ."

"Like I told you, it's not always easy to make it on time."

"I'm beginning to wonder if the fact that we're friends and neighbors isn't getting in the way."

"How's that?"

"Well, since we're friends, it feels to me like you're coming in late, knowing full well that it could be hard for me to hold you accountable. Do I have this right, or am I missing something here?"

Your conclusion could be dead wrong, but it is your conclusion that's starting to eat at you, and now you've done your best to make it safe to talk about it. By taking the attitude that you could be wrong and using tentative language, you're being fair.

Continually Watch for Safety Problems

Warning: Once you start to tell your story, no matter how tentative you are, there's a chance the other person will become defensive. If, for example, you believe your teenage son has stolen money from you, regardless of how tentative you are, you're likely to experience something like this:

YOU: Given that you're the only one who's been in the house in the last four hours and $200 is missing out of my wallet, it's hard for me not to wonder if you took it.

SON: I can't believe you're calling me a thief! *(Stomps out of room and slams door.)*

To handle this level of defensiveness, first, recognize it for what it is: *a threat to safety*. The problem is not that the other person can't handle the content you're offering; it's that he or she doesn't feel safe with you discussing it. When you realize that the problem is one of safety, you'll do the right thing: step out of the content and rebuild safety. Decide whether the problem is that the other person feels disrespected or believes your intentions are bad (or both). Then use the Contrasting skill we described earlier to relieve that person's mind.

YOU: I'm not calling you a thief. I am trying to come up with explanations for what just happened. Can you see how I would wonder given the facts I just described? My intention here is not to accuse you but to find out what is really going on so I can solve this problem. Can we talk about it?

If you start to share your story and the other person becomes defensive, take away his or her fear. Step out of the content and restore safety.

End with a Question

You started the accountability discussion by doing your best to make it safe. You then shared your path in a way that continued to maintain safety. Now it's time to bring your opening paragraph to a close, still maintaining safety. End with a simple diagnostic question: What happened? Make this an honest inquiry, not a veiled threat or an accusation such as "What's wrong with you!"

As you finish off your description of the failed expectation, your goal should be to hear the other person's point of view. If you've started with safety and presented detailed facts, the person responsible for the infraction should understand what the problem is and feel comfortable talking about the underlying cause and the eventual solution.

Don't underestimate the importance of this sincere question. This is a pivotal moment in the conversation, one that will sustain the safety you've created. If you sincerely want to hear the other person's point of view, you let him or her know that this is a dialogue, not a monologue. You help the other person understand that your goal is not to be right or to punish but to solve a problem and that all the information must be out in the open for that to occur. So end your opening statement with a sincere invitation for the other person to share even completely contrary opinions with you.

Finally, as the other person answers the question "What happened?" listen carefully.

Diagnose the root of the problem—which of the six sources of influence is at play? Is the person unmotivated? Is he or she unable? The solution to each alternative is quite different. You don't want to try to motivate people who can't do what you've asked, or enable people who don't care. We'll look at ways to deal with each of these problems in the next two chapters. For now, remember to listen for the underlying cause.

TIPS FOR TOUGH SITUATIONS

Avoid Groundhog Day

Let's return to an element we referred to earlier. It's an important enough issue that it deserves special and repeated attention. As you confront other people, they're likely to want to reduce a performance gap to its simplest form, one that avoids most of what's actually going on and sidesteps the lion's share of accountability. They want to keep treating the problem, no matter how devilishly recurring, as if it were the first instance.

For example, a salesperson who reports to you has a history of promising discounts that cut too deeply into your profits. In short, she sells out profits to earn her commission. Last week you talked to her about this practice, and she agreed to follow the pricing guidelines. Five minutes ago you overheard her deep-discounting again. You step up to the problem:

> *"Louise, I thought we agreed that you wouldn't sell the product below the standard pricing formula. I just over-heard you promising a price that was clearly out of bounds. Did I miss something?"*

Louise explains that she really needed this commission and was hoping that you would understand. Now what?

Moment of Truth

You're now at a critical juncture. You have two problems, not one: (1) the price violation, or the content of the problem, and (2) a whole new problem: she didn't live up to her commitment to you. Many people miss this important difference. Unfortunately, if you talk only about the price formula, you're forced to relive the same problem. Savvy problem solvers know better. As new violations emerge, they step up to them:

> *"Let's see if I understand. You agreed not to cut prices, but you wanted the commission, so you did so anyway. Is that right?"*

This follow-on statement leads to a very different discussion. Instead of talking only about pricing, you're now talking about failing to live up to a commitment. That is a far bigger issue.

Two Examples

To see how the skills we've covered work, here are a couple of examples of how they all come together. We'll start with a simple example: A person who reports to you fails to show up at an important meeting, and you don't think he missed it on purpose.

You have told yourself no story. You invite him into your office, safely describe the gap, and end with a question.

"Chris, I noticed that you missed the meeting you had agreed to attend. I was wondering what happened. Did you run into a problem of some kind?"

And there you have it: a simple paragraph. You haven't held court. You don't have a story to tell. You take the other person to a private setting, describe the facts (what was expected versus what was observed), and end with a question. And now you're listening to diagnose the underlying cause.

Let's examine a tougher problem. You're talking to your boss about what's been happening in meetings. You think he or she may become defensive, so you start by creating safety. You establish Mutual Purpose and use Contrasting.

YOU: I've noticed myself withdrawing in the last couple of meetings. I know it bugs you when I don't take the initiative, so I've thought about why I'm not doing that. Some of the things, I've realized, have to do with how you lead our meetings. I don't want to be presumptuous or tell you how to run meetings, but I believe that if I could discuss this with you, it might help me perform better and would make the climate better for me too. Would that be okay?

BOSS: Okay, what's bugging you?

Since you have told yourself a story about what your boss is doing, you share your path, starting with the facts and then tentatively sharing your conclusion.

YOU: Well, a couple of times in the meeting today when I'd start a comment, you'd raise your hand toward me and then start speaking before I'd finished. I don't know if this is how you mean that, but to me it feels like you think my idea is stupid and it's a way of shutting me down.

BOSS: Yeah, I guess I did do that, but you know, I just don't want to pussyfoot around when I disagree with something. Do I have to?

The boss is feeling defensive, and so you step out of the content and build safety.

YOU: I don't want you to feel like you have to pull punches with me at all. All I'm asking for is that you tell me you disagree in a way that doesn't also sound like you don't think I'm competent. [Contrast.] Is there something I'm doing in the meeting that is irritating you? Or am I not performing up to par and you have concerns about me? [End with a question.]

CHAPTER SUMMARY

Describe the Gap

We've finished working on ourselves and are now speaking for the first time. Our overall goal is to create and maintain safety. Rather than leading with unhealthy conclusions or making accusations (both make it unsafe for the other person), we simply describe the gap. That is, we share our view of what we expected as well as what we actually observed.

We often refer to such breaches as "violated expectations," or "broken commitments." To avoid the harsh conclusions that typically accompany words such as *violated*, or *broken*, we've chosen the more neutral term: *gap*.

When we think of a disappointment as a gap or difference rather than a purposeful violation, we're likely to enter the conversation feeling curious as opposed to feeling disappointed or even angry. By first viewing and then explaining the differences between what was expected and what was observed, we turn the "hazardous half-minute" into a description of the facts (rather than a verbal assault) and show a willingness to learn (rather than a burning desire to accuse). By focusing on the gap, we transform the "hazardous half-minute" into a solid start.

Once we've described the gap, we listen carefully to see which branch of the model we'll pursue. Is the problem due to motivation, ability, or both?

- In this chapter we explored the first words out of our mouth. Our goal has been to make it safer to deal with problems by mastering the critical first moments of an accountability discussion. We've suggested the following:
  - Start with safety.
  - Share your path.
  - End with a question.

- We've written a lot about a little. You don't want to start off on the wrong foot.

Author Video: David Maxfield in "The Law of the Hog"

To watch this and other videos, visit http://www.vitalsmarts .com/bookresources.

What's Next?

The other person is about to explain why he or she let you down. This means that you have to know what to do if the other person isn't motivated or isn't able or maybe both. This will take more than a well-crafted sentence or two.

4

Make It Motivating

How to Help Others Want to Take Action

Let's take a look at where we are in the problem-solving process. Myra, an employee who works for you, failed to complete an important quality check. You observed the gap, decided to deal with it, and tried to determine the right problem to discuss. Since this was the first infraction, you've decided to talk about the content: she didn't complete the quality check. You admire Myra, and so it is easy to impute good motive. Now you describe the gap. After your brief and effective problem description, Myra responds.

REMEMBER TO DIAGNOSE

The way Myra responds to your description of the gap will determine what you do next. She determines your path, not you. You'll learn where you're going by diagnosing the underlying cause of the problem. Is it a matter of motivation, ability, or both? If Myra says, "I couldn't do the procedure you asked for," you'll need to figure out why. Which of the three ability forces is coming into play? If Myra replies, "Come on. What's the big deal? It's a stupid little quality check. I don't really have to do it, do I?" you're staring at a motivation problem. Which of the motivational forces is at work here?

Knowing how to bring to the surface and resolve all the underlying causes requires a great deal of skill. If you miss a single ability barrier, the other person won't be able to cooperate. If you misinterpret the underlying motivational block, you'll be pushing the wrong buttons. You'll also have to choke back the desire to pull out the big guns to motivate (it's so fast and easy) or pull out your big ideas to enable (it's so fast and easy). Both methods are tempting, and both will be wrong.

IT'S ABOUT TO GET COMPLICATED

We begin our journey into the land of multiple causes with a warning: it's about to get complicated. We also offer a promise: if you follow the best practices of those who routinely step up to accountability discussions and handle them well, you too will succeed.

After hemming and hawing for a few seconds, Myra explains that she really didn't *want* to do the job and asks, "What's the big deal? Is it really worth the effort?" From this particular response, we'll conclude that she's not motivated. Other signs that a person isn't motivated include the following: "I had more important things to do." "It wasn't *my* idea to switch jobs." "If you think I'm going to work on something that isn't on my performance review, you're wrong." All point to underlying motive. All imply "I *chose* not to do it."

How do we make it motivating for Myra? How do you reach into other people's psyches regardless of their power or position or, better still, regardless of *your* power or position and motivate them to do what they promised to do?

Hint: Your power doesn't matter all that much. In fact, in many cases the more you think you need power to influence others' motivation, the less likely you are to do it well. Stick with us, and you'll see why.

DON'T OVERSIMPLIFY MOTIVATION: A SMALL RANT

When someone lets you down and does so willfully and with full knowledge of what he or she is doing, you want to deal with the selfish blighter. For instance, remember what your high school boyfriend once did to you? He didn't *forget* to pick you up for your prom date, nor did he come down with a debilitating disease. He simply changed his mind at the last minute. And then, guess what? He said nothing to you, roared by your house in his candy-apple-red Mustang, and then whooped it up with the little hussy who moved in from California while you sat on your front porch clutching a wilted boutonniere.

When it comes to motivating others, these are the thoughtless curs we have in mind. We think of people who have purposely violated a promise and as a result have given us a figurative kick in the gut. Do you know why they cause us grief? Because they don't care. They don't share our wants and needs. They don't walk in our moccasins. When you think about it, isn't that what life comes down to? If we could find a way to get our friends, our family, our coworkers, and especially our boss to climb into our heads, share our dreams, and want what we want, wouldn't life be one great big chocolate croissant?

Motivation with a Capital *M*

When others willfully break a promise, particularly when they cause us loads of grief, we want so desperately to motivate the guilty parties that the whole concept of motivation takes on mythical proportions. We think of motivation with a capital *M*: arm-flailing speeches echoing through a coliseum with the crowd cheering. Or perhaps we envision motivation as the raw use of power delivered in a satisfying and vengeful strike to the ego. Or maybe we think of it as a tool bag chock-full of clever techniques, just underhanded enough to trick people into compliance but sincere-looking enough to maintain a patina of professionalism. And on a good day, maybe our best day, we think of motivation as the ever-popular "art of getting people to do what you want them to do because they want to do it."

Of course, none of these views is particularly helpful. All lead to behaviors that eventually get us into trouble. Even the last cloyingly patronizing statement—we think it's our job to get people to want what we want—is fraught with problems. It works only if we're omniscient (what we want is always right).

At the heart of our twisted view of how to motivate others lies an accumulation of outdated methods and tortured thoughts, one piled upon another. We come to believe that good leaders propel people to action by blending two parts charisma, one part chutzpah, and a healthy dash of fear into a perfect motivational cocktail. And we're wrong.

With time and constant exposure to these unhealthy influence theories, here's what eventually happens to our thinking.

What's with Those Kids?

The apartment you live in comes with a reserved parking space conveniently located right in front of the building's entrance.

Unfortunately, the tenants in the apartment above you have three—count them, three—teenage children, each with a car. They appear to take joy in parking in your place. Each time they compel you to station your vehicle blocks away, you're forced to schlepp yourself over hill and dale through an unrelenting Seattle-style drizzle while you make a mental note to send a generous donation to the National Association to Outlaw Teenagers.

You once talked to both the parents and the adolescents about the problem. You were on your best behavior. You spared no charm, plucked the old heartstrings, and sure enough, they expressed their deepest and most sincere sorrow. It was rather touching. They then respected your parking spot for a full 12 hours, after which they continued with their old tricks. Apparently they were sorry you spoke to them, not sorry that they were causing you problems.

At this point you're fully aware of your options. You know that if you threaten your neighbors, they might come around. But you don't want to be that kind of person. You're bigger than that. So you back off, buy a larger umbrella, and take satisfaction in the knowledge that although you may be drenched and aching, you have not yet mutated into that crotchety old curmudgeon you vowed never to become. Just because you despise these cretins, it doesn't mean you need to be unpleasant about it.

This kind of thinking leads to a false dichotomy. You believe that when it gets right down to it, you must either put up with the current problem or motivate the kids through power and threats; those are the only two options. (Once again, our math is messed up.) And since you don't want to become threatening and abusive, your monklike vow of silence isn't a sellout; it's the moral thing to do.

However, if circumstances demand a more forceful approach, you take comfort in the knowledge that the end will justify the means. After all, it is your parking space, and it's not your fault that the bozos you're dealing with respond only to fear. As long as you believe that the principal motivating force behind all behavior is fear, you have a built-in excuse for going to either silence or violence.

GETTING TO THE ROOT OF MOTIVATION

Contrary to popular myth, you don't have to wield power or provoke fear to be an effective motivator. In fact, it's better if we don't think of ourselves as larger-than-life figures burdened with the challenge of bringing the nearly dead back to life through various inspiring techniques. That kind of flawed thinking is exactly what gets us into trouble.

Consider Melissa, a manager and positive deviant in the large midwestern manufacturing facility we referenced earlier. Weighing about 105 pounds, Melissa was far too small to intimidate anyone, and rarely, if ever, did she use her formal authority or position power. Yet she was extraordinarily influential, singled out by many as being the most effective manager in the facility. In fact, the amount of power you have has little to do with how well you motivate others. We have watched people with almost no authority motivate their bosses' bosses.

Motivation, it turns out, is actually rather boring. It has little to do with clout or charisma. In fact, motivation is about expectations, information, and communication.

Expectations Change Everything

Let's start our more accurate, if less flamboyant, description of motivation with a simple truism: people are always motivated. To say that someone isn't motivated is patently wrong. As long as people are moving their muscles, they're motivated to do *something*. Second, motivation is brain driven. People choose their behavior. Third, motivation is influenced by a nearly infinite number of sources from both within and without.

Here's how the human brain and the surrounding world combine to propel individual behavior. Human beings anticipate. When deciding what to do, they look to the future and ask, "What will this particular behavior yield?" When they choose one action over another, it's because they're betting that that action will generate the best result. Since any action yields a combination of results, some good and some bad, it's the expected sum total of the *consequence bundle* that drives behavior. If you want people to act in another way, you have to let them know how a different behavior would yield a better consequence bundle.

> Here's what motivation comes down to: change others' view of the consequence bundle, and their behavior will follow.

How do you help people to change their view of the consequence bundle—to understand that their existing view is either inaccurate or incomplete?

THREE APPROACHES TO AVOID

One thing is for certain: three of the more popular methods— charisma, power, and perks—don't work very well. They all have the potential to change people's view, and so they all have the potential to change people's behavior. Unfortunately, relying on these heavy-handed methods can be dangerous and rarely sustains behavior over the long run. Yet these methods remain enormously popular. In fact, they hold a nearly sacred place in the leadership lexicon. Let's consider each method in turn.

Don't Rely on Charisma

It's time to kill a myth. To be an effective motivator, you don't have to be awe inspiring. Everyday acts of motivation are almost always subtle, rarely elicit awe, and never make the papers. Nevertheless, the myth of charisma continues to thrive. Books, television programs, and movies positively ooze with scenes that are designed to make audiences gasp with admiration. For example, in the cold war drama *Crimson Tide*, we find a naval officer played by Denzel Washington giving a "big speech" to a young radioman on whose skill and attention hangs the fate of the world.

The poor fellow has to get the submarine's radio up and running to learn if the vessel should launch its missiles. If he fails, the captain will be forced to launch the sub's nuclear arms blindly, cause the enemy to retaliate, and eventually destroy the world—even though it may not be necessary. ("Sorry. My bad!")

In the real world the poor fellow probably would collapse from the pressure. In fact, the stress would be so debilitating that a smart leader would be doing everything in his or her power to provide support. But screenwriters are human too. They make the fundamental attribution error by creating a radioman who doesn't need support. He needs to be inspired. Apparently, he hasn't repaired the radio yet because he has something he'd rather do than save the world from total destruction.

Denzel delivers a really hot speech. After the tear-jerking performance, the radioman turns to his coworker and tells him to stop messing around so that they can prevent a nuclear holocaust instead of playing video games or whatever it is they're doing.

Denzel gives the speech, the radioman is appropriately inspired, and, yes, the audience breaks into applause. Charisma makes for good drama; however, it has precious little to do with real leadership. Rest assured that you don't have to be charismatic to be influential.

Don't Use Power

Let's move on to the next big mistake. Raw power, painfully applied, may move bodies, it may even get people to act in new ways, but it rarely moves hearts and minds. Hearts and minds are changed through expanded understanding and new realizations.

The flagrant and abusive use of authority, in contrast, guarantees little more than short-term bitter compliance.

This simple idea would never have made these pages if not for the fact that parents and leaders alike routinely turn to power as their *first* tool for motivating others. Without putting it in so many words, they believe that it's easiest to change people's thinking about the existing consequence bundle by administering new and painful consequences of their own. It's a simple enough concept and is very easy to implement. Here's what it sounds like:

- "If you don't finish the project on time, you're fired!"

- "If you talk back to me like that again, you're grounded until the end of the summer!"

The Reason We Intuitively Rely on Force

Earlier we suggested that we often take a dispositional rather than a situational view of others. If others cause us a great deal of pain, we believe they must be bad to the core. The worse the impact others have on us, the worse our assumptions about their character. We think they're inherently selfish. They may even take joy in our suffering. They're at best indifferent. And here's where it gets sticky: We believe that others are *capable* only of being selfish. It's in their genes. It's their disposition. It's not a choice; it's a calling.

When it comes to influence strategies, the implication of this dispositional view of people should be obvious. Individuals aren't going to change their personalities through patience and long suffering on our part. They're not going to change their proverbial spots after we give them an inspiring pep talk. In fact, they aren't going to change their inherent and immutable personalities because of anything we say. They can't.

And now for a leap in logic that would break any Evel Knievel record: since we're dealing with deep-seated personality flaws, we have to use threats. Remember those teenagers who took your parking space? Oh yeah, they'll pay.

Warning: You're About to Do Something Stupid

What does all this chest beating come down to? Let's take it as a warning. The more we feel the need to apply force, the greater is the evidence that our own thoughts are the problem. To quote *Seinfeld*'s George Costanza, "It's not them, it's us."

Of course, it starts with them when they aren't motivated. We try and try, and nothing works. And then we become angry. We convince ourselves that we need to use power to solve the problem, and we enjoy doing it. That's because we're thinking with our dumbed-down, adrenaline-fed lizard brains.

> Warning lights should go off every time we feel compelled to reach into our bag of influence tools and pull out a hammer: if we don't catch ourselves before it's too late, we'll pay.

The Cost of Force

Force Kills Relationships

Every time we decide to use our power to influence others, particularly if we're gleeful and hasty, we damage the relationship. We move from enjoying a healthy partnership based on trust and Mutual Respect to establishing a police state that requires constant monitoring.

Every time we compel people to bend to our will, it creates a desolate and lonely work environment. Gone is Mutual Respect and the camaraderie it engenders. Gone are the simple pleasantries associated with rubbing shoulders with colleagues who admire and pull for each other. Gone is the sense that we're laboring together to overcome common barriers.

It's a horrible thing we do when we decide to unleash our power as a method of motivating others. When we do, our relationship with others is forever changed. We move from respected partner to feared enforcer. And then we pay.

Force Motivates Resistance

When we quickly move to use force to influence change, people intuitively understand that we do that because we believe they have bad motives. We don't respect them. In addition, it communicates that we care only about *our* goals, not theirs. In other words, it destroys safety. And when safety disappears, people immediately become defensive. Eventually they resist our ideas out of principle. Every time we leave the room, we wonder if they'll actually do what we've asked. By destroying safety, the hasty use of force ensures that force will be needed to solve the problem and that a healthy accountability discussion won't work.

Force Doesn't Last

Back in the mid-1930s, Kurt Lewin, along with several of his colleagues, conducted a fascinating study that forever put to rest the notion that exercising one's power yields lasting results. The researchers randomly assigned leaders to one of three leadership styles: authoritarian, hands-off, and democratic. The subjects then used their assigned styles to lead a production team. As expected, the authoritarian (power-based) style produced the highest results when the leader was in the room. Also as expected, force yielded the lowest results once the leader left the room.[1] When people produce solely out of fear, once the fear is removed, so is the motivation to continue to follow orders.

Be Careful with Perks

Now for the last of the common motivational errors: the hasty use of extrinsic rewards to motivate what should already be intrinsically motivating. Many parents have learned not to make this mistake through their failed attempts to reward actions that should be rewarding in and of themselves.

For example, if you want your children to read or, better still, *love* to read, what's the best way to lure them away from their electronic devices? More than a few parents have chosen to pay their kids to read. The theory is that if you pay them, they'll read, and if they read, they'll learn to love reading. Unfortunately, extrinsic rewards often kill intrinsic satisfaction. These children learn to read for money, not for the love of reading. Then the minute the cash is removed, they're off books.

Similarly, if you continually use special perks to encourage people to do what should be a routine part of their jobs, in effect "perfuming" the consequence bundle, you could be undermining or even destroying the satisfaction that comes from doing the job. It also takes attention away from the legitimate reasons for the work. When extrinsic rewards are applied to routine behavior, they confuse purpose. Special rewards should be reserved for special performance.

THE SOLUTION

The problem with power, perks, and charisma is not that they never work or never should be used. The problem is that people turn to them too quickly, and there are almost always better methods. For instance, savvy parents and influential leaders use their ability to teach. They intuitively instruct by using part of the model we developed in Chapter 2.

Explore Natural Consequences

When you watch people who have been singled out by their bosses, peers, and loved ones as the best at handling accountability discussions (those highly valued positive deviants we introduced earlier), it should be no surprise to learn that they change people's hearts by changing their minds.

Savvy leaders recognize that they could propel people to action by using their leadership authority or offering perks. They also know that within the three domains of personal, social, and structural, there are other factors that are far better motivators, that propel action without the leader pulling strings or making threats.

What are these compelling factors? They are the *natural* consequences associated with any behavior. For example, if you don't manage your diabetes well, you are likely to face amputations later in life. That's a natural consequence. If you fail to follow up on commitments, you create extra stress for your boss, who has to guess what will get done. That's a natural consequence. If you make sarcastic and cutting comments when your spouse isn't feeling amorous, she will withdraw and feel less spontaneous affection for you despite what your lizard brain is telling you. That's a natural consequence.

All our actions put into play a chain of events that affects anywhere from one person to millions of other people. This sequence of events makes up the consequence bundle. Among these consequences, there is a subset of "natural" consequences that exist independently of the intervention of an authority figure. These methods require no force, no chutzpah, and no charisma. No parent has to wag a finger; no boss has to write up a disciplinary action. Natural consequences are always present and always serve as a potential source of motivation.

Of course, not all natural consequences motivate people equally. Here is an example:

> *"When you cut Jimmy off in midsentence, it hurt his feelings."*
> *"Good, I don't like him anyway."*

> Consequences provide the force behind all behavioral choices, and so savvy influencers motivate others by completing a consequence search: they explain natural consequences until they hit upon one or more that the other person values. As you start your own consequence search, your job is to find a way to make the invisible visible while maintaining healthy dialogue.

Make the Invisible Visible

When it comes to exploring natural consequences, your primary responsibility is to help others see consequences they aren't seeing (or remembering) on their own. That happens because many of the outcomes associated with a particular behavior are long term or occur out of sight. Your job is to help make the invisible visible. Here are six methods for doing that.

Link to Existing Values

As you consider all the consequences you could discuss with another person, turn your attention to that person's core values. What does he or she care about the most? This will be your point of greatest leverage. Then help the other person see how his or her values will be better supported through the course you are proposing. If you have created enough safety, you can talk frankly about any value issues. Let's look at an example of speaking with a spouse who has had two bypass surgeries and continues to gorge:

> *"Dear, I honestly believe that if your eating habits don't change, you won't raise our children; I will. Do you have the same concern? What do you think?"*

Here you're trying to deal with your loved one's eating habits, and rather than nagging or attacking, you're linking to his or her core value of being around to help raise the kids.

Connect Short-Term Benefits with Long-Term Pain

Show how the short-term enjoyment the person currently is experiencing is inextricably connected to longer-term problems. This is essentially the central task of parenting:

> *"If you continue to watch television and don't do your homework, you'll get bad grades, you won't get into a good school, you won't get a good job, you won't make lots of money, and you'll never drive your own Porsche."*

You might not use this whole list (you're piling on), but this is at least part of the map you're carrying in your head and the map you'd like your child to share eventually, except maybe the part about the fancy car.

This method of clarifying long-term or distant negative consequences is also applied at work dozens of times a day:

> *"I'm sure it's a hassle to double-check appointments when you enter them on my calendar, but our current error rate is so high that the assistants of the other vice presidents are calling me to ask for confirmation. I worry that your reputation here is going to be hurt if we can't solve this."*

Place the Focus on Long-Term Benefits

This is the other half of parenting. It's also the single best predictor of lifelong success. If a person can suffer a little now—delaying gratification in order to serve a longer-term goal—life gets better (think dieting, weight training, studying, etc.).

If you doubt this premise, consider a study conducted over a matter of decades. A researcher put a marshmallow in front of individual children and told them that they would get another one if they didn't eat the first one while the researcher stepped out. As the researchers tracked these children over the years, they found that those who had waited for the researchers to return did far better in life than those who ate the confection right away, and in almost every domain.[2] To help people stay the course, take the focus off the short-term challenge by placing it on the long-term benefit:

"I know that putting up with some of the kids' messiness is really hard for you. I also believe that your relationship with them is at risk if you can't learn to let some of the smaller things go."

Introduce the Hidden Victims

This is perhaps the most widely used method of explaining consequences. You describe the unintended and often invisible effects an action is having on others. At work, leaders carefully and clearly explain the consequences to the company's various stakeholders:

"Here's what your failure to comply is doing to other employees, to the customer, to the shareowners, to the boss, and so forth."

At home, parents explain what's happening to other family members:

"Louisa, I know your little brother gets on your nerves a lot. But did you know that when you made fun of his

weight, he sat in his room and cried for the rest of the eve-
ning? I know your goal was to get him to stop following
you around and not to hurt him so deeply. Is that right?"

Hold Up a Mirror

To help introduce the social implications of a particular action, describe how a person's action is being viewed by others. "It's starting to look like you don't care about the team's results." Remember, when it comes to the way we're coming across, we all live on the wrong side of our eyeballs. Help others gain a view from the other side.

Connect to Existing Rewards

This is typically not the best starting place, but eventually you may want to talk about rewards. Help others see how living up to an expectation advances their careers, enhances their influence, puts more money in the bank, or reduces their risks:

> *"You've mentioned wanting to be the art director. In my*
> *view you will be much more successful in that position—*
> *and more likely to get it—if you have a solid working rela-*
> *tionship with both the editing staff and the video team."*

Stay in the Conversation

Remember, as you're doing your best to make consequences more visible, keep talking. Keep the information flowing honestly and freely in both directions.

Don't Turn Consequences into Threats

There's a fine line between sharing natural consequences and threatening others. Well, in most cases it's not that fine a line. If your motives are wrong, sharing becomes threatening. If your motive is to punish or if you're taking pleasure in describing the awful things that will happen if someone's obnoxious behavior continues, you're making threats. Your motive must be to solve the problem in a way that benefits both of you. Anything less than that will provoke silence or violence, not gain willing compliance.

The challenge increases when your motives are right but the other person mistakes your description of natural consequences for a threat. "When you fail to complete your assignments on time, we start giving you less relevant assignments to protect ourselves from failure" can sound like a personal attack or a job threat.

If the other person believes that he or she is in trouble, perhaps because of previous experience with other bosses, your best behavior may seem manipulative regardless of your skill or demeanor. If you notice that others appear nervous, step out of the conversation and restore safety by explaining your positive intentions. Explain that your goal is to solve an important problem. You simply want to share the consequences of what they're doing and then ask them for their view on the matter. When they start hearing natural consequences as threats, you should recognize the situation as a safety problem and restore safety.

Listen to Others' View of Natural Consequences

When it comes to other people's roles, you should be listening as they explain their view of the consequences. They may be aware of consequences you know little or nothing about: "Yeah, we can do it the way you want, but it'll blow up our lawn mower."

Your view of what should be done may change in the process of jointly discussing consequences. In the end, you may be convinced that they *shouldn't* do what you originally asked.

Stop When You Reach Compliance

As you help others see consequences they didn't realize existed, explain those consequences only until you believe others will comply. Your job isn't to keep piling on information. It is to share consequences until the other person understands the overall effect and shares your view of what needs to be done. Don't sell past the close.

Match Methods to Circumstances

Let's look at the final element of making a task motivating. It has to do with the circumstances you're facing. Sometimes the person you're talking to is simply unaware of the consequences associated with his or her actions. Sometimes you yourself don't understand why the other person isn't motivated. Or perhaps the person is partially motivated but the task just hasn't made it to the top of his or her priority list. Maybe the other person's openly resisting your efforts. Let's learn to match method to circumstance.

When You're Teaching

The methods for explaining natural consequences that we've just examined are easy to apply when we're first informing people about the reason behind a specific action. Employees want to know why they have to produce products and deliver services by using certain methods—particularly if what you're asking isn't going to be easy. What they really want to know is whether it's actually worth the effort. As we suggested earlier, individuals who are good at accountability are teachers, and much of their teaching is about the consequences to varying stakeholders: "Here's why it's worth it." They make the invisible visible by whatever means will work.

When it comes to parenting, the younger the child, the greater the need to teach the child the relationship between behavior and outcome. Newborns do not understand consequences. Almost everything a parent does during the early stages of child rearing is to protect a child from invisible bad consequences and then to teach. As children grow older, methods change and resistance increases, at least until age 14, when your offspring actually know everything and you don't have to teach them anymore. Of course, when they turn 21, they become ignorant again.

When You're Jointly Exploring

This circumstance comes up more often than you might imagine. The other person isn't exactly motivated, and neither of you is quite sure why. Perhaps the other person knows why but isn't saying. In either case, you can't figure out why the other person isn't motivated, and you'll need to examine the impact that personal, social, and structural factors are having on the individual to determine which ones are making the task undesirable.

The idea here is to examine each source of influence with simple questions: "Is the job hard to do?" "Is it repetitive, boring, uncomfortable (and so on)? Is that why you don't want to do it?" "Are others encouraging you not to do it?" "Is the task at odds with what the other person is getting rewarded for?"

> The goal of exploring consequences is to bring to the surface the issues that make the task undesirable. If it's not immediately clear, this could take some work. Once you're both aware of the factors that are at play, decide if you still want the other person to continue (you may change your mind). If you decide that the task still makes sense, use any combination of the methods we've described for making the consequences visible.

When Priorities Differ

What if the other person has different priorities? It's not that people don't want to do the task; it's just not at the top of their list. Priorities can differ for several reasons. Maybe other tasks came up out of nowhere, or perhaps that person enjoys doing other jobs more. Maybe the people who have let you down have forgotten what they were supposed to do or, more likely, why they were supposed to do it. Here's a big one: perhaps they were hoping that nobody would care if they dropped that part of the job. They eliminated it and watched to see what would happen.

Whatever the reason, people know what to do but choose something else. Let's be honest: more often than not, they already know what the consequences will be. Under these circumstances, explaining why certain parts of the job are necessary can sound quite different from routine instruction. You're now doing your best to *remind* people without haranguing them. Consider the following:

> *"Are you sure that I need to explain safety procedures to everyone walking in here? Some of the visitors have been here before."*
>
> *"Remember when we had that discussion a couple of months back about government regulations? If people get hurt, they can sue us if we haven't talked to them every time. I know it can seem redundant, but it's the law."*

Reminding people is the tactic you take with hardworking, reliable individuals who are caught in a priority battle.

When Others Resist

Let's consider a more challenging case. Individuals are openly resisting your efforts. They really don't want to fulfill their promise, they need to be convinced, and you need to be careful not to create resistance. That means that you'll need to know how to explain why something has to be done without jumping straight to power or discipline. Now what?

This is the discussion people have in mind when they say that those they work and live with are hard to motivate: "Others fight me at every turn." Fortunately, the basic principle is the same: explain natural consequences until the person genuinely agrees to comply. In this case it's a delicate search. You keep searching for consequences until you find one the other person values. Here are examples:

> *"Come on. I have better things to do than get my expense reports in the day I get back."*
>
> *"We've found that the longer people drag it out, the less accurate their reports are. They often forget small expenses, and it costs them money"* (consequences to the employee).
>
> *"I've got a good memory."*
>
> *"It also causes trouble for the people in accounting. They have their own deadlines and goals. If we wait too long, it throws them off"* (consequences to coworkers).
>
> *"Big deal. Let them suffer once in a while. I'm the one on the road half my life."*
>
> *"When you don't get your bills in, we don't bill our clients as quickly. Last year we figure late billing cost the company over $200,000"* (consequences to shareholders).
>
> *"We made a bazillion dollars last year."*
>
> *"When you drag out your reports for a couple of weeks, I get a call, and I have to track you down and hold these kinds of conversations. It's not how I want to spend my time"* (consequences to the boss).
>
> *"Hmmm. I didn't realize I was making more work for you. Sorry. From now on I'll put a reminder in my calendar, and it'll keep me on track."*

This type of lengthy consequence search calls for both patience and skill. The person really doesn't want do what you're asking, and it takes a genuine search to come up with something that motivates him or her. You have to search because not every consequence matters to everyone. In this example the employee didn't care about anything until the boss talked about how it was inconveniencing him (which, by the way, implies the use of power).

When to Use Discipline

Despite your best efforts, sometimes you still have to start down the path of discipline. Perhaps the other person has done something that requires immediate action. Maybe your son crossed the line from resisting your efforts to being disrespectful and insulting. Maybe you've explained consequences, and the other person isn't going to do what you ask no matter what you say.

Perhaps you've had multiple conversations—describing content, pattern, and relationship—but the employee is still violating every agreement you make. It's time to change tactics. It's time to move away from natural consequences and start imposing consequences of your own (discipline). As you start down this precarious path, keep the following in mind.

Know the Mechanics

Every organization has its own discipline steps and policies. Study them carefully. If you fail to follow procedure, your efforts may be thrown out when they are reviewed, undermining your credibility. Families should create their own clear disciplinary steps as well. If they do not, everything comes as a surprise.

Partner with People in Authority

If you're in a situation in which you don't know the person's total history and details, explain why the action was wrong, state that you're going to move to discipline, and say that you'll get back to him or her later. Then check with specialists to learn what the actual steps should be. Otherwise you may suggest that you're going to send the person home without pay and then find out that he or she was only due for a warning. You'll have to eat your words. The home version of this should be obvious: parents must be unified in their actions.

Be Appropriately Somber

Discipline isn't something you impose with a sense of pleasure regardless of what the other person may have done. Keep the tone serious and speak about what has to be done, not what you now get to do. This is not a time for a smug in-your-face celebration. You're moving from leading or partnering to policing, and that's hardly a victory.

Explain the Next Step

As you explain what will happen as a result of the infraction, cover what will happen if the person does the same thing again. Explaining the next level of consequences informs and motivates. It also helps eliminate surprises: "Nobody said I was going to be fired!"

Be Consistent

Don't play favorites. If you're working with an employee who gives you fits at every turn, you can't discipline that person for something you wouldn't discipline everyone for simply as a means of getting even. When discipline falls under review, the first thing third parties examine is equity. Did the person get fair treatment? Don't single people out.

Don't Back Off Under Pressure

Once you've started the process, stick to it. Follow the steps and don't be dissuaded simply because the person puts up a fight. If discipline is called for, stay the course. If you waffle, you'll gain a reputation for making hollow threats.

When Power Fails, Be Candid About Coping

Let's look at one final issue. What if you've explained the natural consequences associated with an action but others still aren't motivated and you can't or shouldn't impose consequences to increase their motivation? Let's say your boss realizes he should stop yelling at you and others but says the following: "I know it's wrong, I know it frustrates people, but I'm high-strung and under a lot of pressure, and it's just going to happen sometimes!" Now what? You're not likely to impose consequences on your boss.

Or let's say your business partner has been unreliable in getting assignments in on time, and after a lengthy discussion you still believe it's likely she'll get them in late. What do you do?

Agree on a Work Around

When you've decided not to administer discipline as a way of compelling someone to change his or her actions, develop a coping strategy and then candidly share it. That way, as the other person observes and experiences the consequences of the work around, he or she can choose to act differently to avoid the pain, waste, and inefficiency you've talked about.

For instance, from this point on you will not give your unreliable partner "critical-path" assignments. She may not be happy about this choice because she wants to be involved with the hottest assignments. Nevertheless, at least she understands why you're doing what you're doing.

With an emotionally explosive boss who refuses to change, you might suggest that when he blows off steam, you'll eventually withdraw, allow time for him to calm down, and then return for a healthier and more complete discussion. You might also share that you are likely to be reluctant to challenge some of his more vigorous arguments. You'll do your best to be candid, but his defensive actions will continue to make that difficult for you. By being candid about your coping strategy, you empower your boss to choose whether he wants this consequence bundle.

This point is so important that we want to expand it a bit. For people to behave badly over the long haul, *we* have to do two things. First, we have to avoid accountability discussions. By doing that, we avoid helping others see the consequences of their behavior. If we don't alter their expectations, why should they change what they do? Second, we create a work-around that enables others to continue doing what they're doing, unaware and guilt free. For example, our boss never returns calls, and so we secretly assign someone to do it for her. A doctor is incompetent, and so we discreetly schedule complicated surgeries for when he's off shift. Our dad is grumpy and abusive, and so we buy him his own wide-screen TV and build him a den.

> The reason others aren't motivated to change is often because of us. We're conspirators. Either we misuse power and mobilize others' resistance, or we withhold honest feedback and then take great pains to create clever and secret work-arounds that continue to keep others blind to the consequences they're causing.

Even if you don't have the power to impose your will on an unwilling person, you can avoid being part of the problem by being candid about your coping strategy.

FINISH WELL

Let's assume you've been able to make it motivating. You jointly discussed consequences, you chose not to back off, and the other person has agreed to comply. The conversation is winding down.

But you're not through. You have to do one more thing to ensure that you haven't wasted your time. Coming to an agreement is one thing; deciding what's going to happen from this point on requires one more step.

As you wrap up the conversation, make a plan. Decide who will do what and by when. Then set a follow-up time in which you can check to see how things are going. (We'll examine how to do this in Chapter 7.)

A FINAL CASE: CAN THIS MARRIAGE BE SAVED?

Let's take a look at how discussing natural consequences applies to a difficult example.

He Hates My Kids

This is both Gary and Kali's second marriage. She has two children from her previous marriage, ages 15 and 20. When Kali and Gary first met, he was very interested in her children. They've now been married four years, and his interest is waning. In fact, he's almost always surly with them and has taken to calling them names. They feel like strangers in the house, and Kali is beginning to think she'll have to choose between Gary and her children.

What makes this problem particularly hard to solve is the fact that *he doesn't want to talk about it*. When Kali tries to discuss their relationship, he accuses her of being unreasonable and storms out of the room. What can she say? One thing is for certain—the first few seconds will be critical. Kali has about 30 seconds to do two things: she has to help Gary want to talk to her, and she has to make it safe so that he'll talk to her constructively. Let's watch her in action. Gary is doing e-mail in the den alone. The kids aren't around, and so they're likely to have an hour or so without interruptions.

KALI: "I think the kids and I are making life unpleasant for you. It appears to be getting worse and not better." *(Make it safe: She maintains respect and clarifies her purpose.)*

"I want to find an hour when we can discuss this. And I believe that if we do, we could get back some of the feeling we shared until about a year ago." *(She provides more safety and Mutual Purpose.)*

"If we don't talk, I don't think we'll be able to continue in the same way." *(She makes the invisible visible, sharing natural consequences that Gary cares about.)*

GARY: "Is that a threat?" *(He mistakes her last statement as emotional blackmail.)*

KALI: "No, and I'm sorry if it sounded like one. I don't want you to feel like I'm attacking you. I just want us to be able to talk openly about something I'm really concerned about." *(She steps out of the content and restores safety using Contrasting.)*

"Let's face it, you and I haven't felt affectionate toward each other in months. I think it's been bad for both of us. I think the problems are solvable, but not if we can't talk about them." *(She shares natural consequences, links to existing values, takes the focus off short-term pain—a conversation—and focuses on long-term benefits.)*

"The conversation doesn't have to happen now, but I believe it must happen or the things that are wrong are just going to get worse. I fear that's likely to end with us feeling like we'd be happier apart than together." *(She connects short-term benefits—avoiding the conversation—with long-term pain.)*

"I hate that thought." *(She steps out of content and makes sure he doesn't mistake the natural consequence for a threat.)*

GARY: "Okay, I'll try. But if this turns into you telling me how I can't expect the kids to obey any rules and I just have to put up with their trashing the house, I'm gone." *(He's moving to violence—making threats—because he doesn't feel safe. He still suspects this will be a blaming conversation with him as the target. Kali recognizes the lack of safety and avoids reacting to his threat. Instead, she increases safety.)*

KALI: "I know I've been doing a lot of that. And I'm sorry. I've been very defensive about the kids lately, and that's come out as me blaming you and not listening to your concerns. I think if we can talk about all of this, we can work together better. Is now a good time?"

GARY: "It's as good as any, I guess. Where do we start?"

CHAPTER SUMMARY

Make It Motivating

We've carefully described the gap and are now listening to see if the problem is due to motivation or ability. In this chapter, we examined the motivational side of the model.

When the other person isn't motivated, it's our job to make the right behavior motivating.

- *Consequences motivate.* Motivation isn't something you do to someone. People already want to do things. They're motivated by the consequences they anticipate. And since any action leads to a variety of consequences, people act on the basis of the overall consequence bundle.

- *Explore natural consequences.* Begin by explaining natural consequences. Within a business context, this typically includes what's happening to stakeholders. Stakeholders include other employees, customers, shareowners, communities, and regulatory agencies.

- *Match method to circumstances.* When people simply want to know, explain both what needs to be done and why. When dealing with someone who is pushing back, resist the temptation to jump to power. Search for consequences that matter to the other person.

- *Finish well.* Finally, wrap up the conversation by determining who does what and by when. Then set a follow-up time.

Additional Resources

Struggling to "make it motivating"? Refer to Appendix C, "When Thing Go Right," for tips on motivating with praise. Also, visit http://www.vitalsmarts.com/bookresources and learn how you can submit your specific questions to the authors of *Crucial Accountability*.

What's Next?

Let's expand our skills to include the other half of our Six-Source Model. Let's learn what to do when the other person is motivated but unable to act.

5

> *Ability will never catch up
> with the demand for it.*
>
> —Confucius

Make It Easy

*How to Make
Keeping Commitments
(Almost) Painless*

It's time to move to the ability side of our model. We'll start with an example. Kyle, a political analyst who works for you, was supposed to write a position paper for an upcoming debate and have it on your desk by noon, but he didn't. You call him in for a private discussion and describe the gap. He lets you know that he really wanted to do what he promised and says that it wasn't his fault that he didn't. The specialist who conducts the statistical analysis was hospitalized with a burst appendix, and she's the only one who understands the data.

In any case, Kyle was prevented from doing what he agreed to do. And then he did exactly the right thing: He immediately called to let you know about the problem, but you were in a meeting across town. He left a message on your voice mail and then tried to track you down. In short, he wasn't able to meet his commitment and did his best to let you know. This was definitely not a motivation problem.

DON'T MISDIAGNOSE

Having just read the last chapter, you decide it would be a good idea to tell Kyle about the natural consequences of missing the deadline. You figure that he needs to know, so you share:

> *"Let me tell you something. If people ask the wrong questions at the debate, we're going to look like a bunch of dopes because we don't have the position paper."*

Kyle turns ashen, mumbles something about tracking down the specialist, and dashes off like a scared rabbit.

"Now he's really motivated!" you think to yourself.

We hope you wouldn't actually do this. Being the steely-eyed smart person you are, you would note that Kyle was motivated to do the job. Piling on more reasons for doing something he wasn't able to do in the first place would be the wrong cure. Indeed, it would be cruel. Kyle needs help removing the barriers he's facing, not a kick in the pants, and so that's where we'll turn. What does it take to help others remove any and all barriers they face? Better still, what can we do to make it easy, even painless, for others to complete their assignments?

Motivation and Ability Are Inextricably Linked

To learn how to enable others, let's start by examining two of the more subtle aspects of motivation and ability. First, motivation and ability are linked at the hip. They aren't separate entities. More often than not, they blend into one another. Here's why. If something is hard to do—perhaps noxious and boring—it's demotivating. Who really *wants* to muck out a horse stall? Or fill out expense reports? Or write a term paper?

Here's our first question: If a job is difficult or revolting or tedious, does this constitute an ability problem or a motivation problem? The person is not able to do the task, at least not easily, and as a result is not motivated to do it. What are we looking at here?

By the purest definition, if individuals can do a job but are not doing it, it's because they aren't motivated. The metaphorical test that people often apply to this question is "If you held a gun to their head, could they do it?" If the answer is yes, they're able but unmotivated.

This simplistic yet violent test doesn't serve us well. If a job is truly impossible, it's a clear-cut ability problem. That's an easy call. For instance, Kyle tried his best to finish his project but was prevented from finishing on time. This had nothing to do with motivation. However, if a task is difficult, disgusting, or dreary, we need to think of the problem in a more complex way. It's not pure ability. It is a composite problem with both motivational and capability components.

Here's how the two elements come together. In the short run, if a task is undesirable but not impossible, we can crank up the pressure and get the job done. Over the long run, we want to find a way to remove some of the factors that make the job undesirable, or we'll constantly be looking for ways to motivate people to do what they hate doing. And that's never fun.

Motivation and Ability Can Be Confused

Here's another concept to keep in mind. When diagnosing the cause, we have to be dead certain that we haven't confused motivation and ability. As completely different as the two things are, people don't always make it easy for us to tell whether they don't want to do what's been asked or can't do it. In fact, we pretty much assume that if we ask nicely enough, people will tell us straight out whether they *couldn't* complete an assignment, they *wouldn't*, or both.

For instance, Wanda, a service-repair technician who works for you, doesn't show up at a client's office. You ask what happened, and she comes back with "I went there, but the doors were locked. I used my cell phone to check what was going on and got voice mail."

It was a clear-cut ability problem. When you're lucky, people come right out and tell you if a problem was due to motivation or ability.

Ambiguous Cause

But you're not always that lucky. More often than you'd like, the other person (in this case, Wanda) comes back with something such as "You know; stuff came up."

This response is just ambiguous enough to be dangerous. You need to probe for *can't* or *won't*. With this in mind, you ask, "Are you saying that you ran into a problem or that you didn't want to do it?"

Wanda continues to baffle you by saying, "You know how it is. I just never got around to it."

You probe one more time: "I'm not sure what you're saying. Did you choose not to do it, or were you unable to do it?"

Complicated Cause

Finally Wanda fesses up. She tells you why, and as is often the case, it's complicated: "I hate working for those guys. They look over my shoulder and complain the whole time. They give me the creeps. I was hoping if I didn't show up, you'd schedule someone else."

There you have it: she didn't *want* to do it (for understandable reasons), shirked the job, didn't let you know, left the client hanging, and was hoping that you'd reward her by sending someone else to the tough client. She chose not to do it (motivation), and as is often the case, she was not all that motivated because she was not all that able. She didn't know how to deal with a tough client.

You'd probably start this conversation with the fact that she chose not to do the job, left the client high and dry, and hoped you'd somehow look the other way. That's a serious infraction. You might eventually work with Wanda to help her get better at dealing with tough clients, but you're not likely to start there. In any case, this problem, like most, is fairly complicated and requires a detailed diagnosis and multiple solutions. Without going into all the sources, you're only going to be able to deal with a subset of the underlying causes.

Masked Cause

Believe it or not, sometimes people purposely hide the genuine source of a problem. If they fear that they'll get in trouble for not being able or not wanting to do what's been asked, they may stretch the truth to avoid new problems. For example, an attending physician asks a medical student to insert an intravenous line into the chest of a 75-year-old patient. The student isn't quite sure how to do it, but when the doctor is called away to work on a cardiac arrest, the student says nothing. Instead, he attempts to insert the line and punctures the sac around the woman's lung, and the patient later dies of related complications. A woman dies because the student is uncomfortable saying that he just might be unable to do what he's been asked. (This actually happened.)

Perhaps the most common ability problem that people try to hide is their illiteracy (23 percent of the population is illiterate). Employees fear they'll lose their jobs if they admit that they can't read or do basic math. You ask, "John, how come you didn't set up the new equipment?" John couldn't read the directions, tried his best, and failed. He thinks he'll be fired if you find out that he can't read, and so he answers, "I hate doing that kind of stuff. It has all those fancy numbers and charts and things—not that I couldn't do it if I wanted to."

If you interpret this response to mean that John doesn't like doing the task, you'll want to explain the natural consequences: "John, we have two clients waiting on the job, and the longer you take getting the equipment up, the longer they'll have to wait."

This, of course, is a doomed conversation, because no matter how many consequences you explain, John is still stuck.

As strange as this may sound, it's not uncommon to discover that employees who are being disciplined for excessive resistance or even insubordination are hiding the fact that they couldn't do what they had been asked to do. They chose discipline over shame or, worse, what they believe is the possibility of being fired.

Probably the most common form of masking takes place when people cover up their lack of motivation with a bogus ability problem. This often occurs when a person figures the boss doesn't really care what happens but then the boss shows up wanting to know why the job wasn't done. Suddenly an ability block sounds better than saying, "I didn't make it a priority." Thus, people come up with whoppers like these:

"I would have been here for the early meeting, but my alarm didn't go off."

"I would have mowed the yard before your lawn party but was wondering if maybe I should cut it shorter than usual."

It's important to listen carefully to the answers to your diagnostic questions. When John states, "It's got all those fancy numbers and charts and things—not that I couldn't do it if I wanted to," a careful person might continue probing about difficulty, making it safe for John to say that he has trouble with the directions.

In responding to bogus motivation problems, it's common to give the person the benefit of the doubt the first time: "So what are you going to do to ensure that your alarm goes off next time?"

If excuses keep cropping up, you have to deal with the pattern as in this example:

"This is the third time you've run into some kind of problem. We've been patient, but the fact is, you have to make those early meetings."

"The last five times I asked you to do a chore around the house, you agreed, I left on an errand, and then you came up with questions and didn't do the job."

YOUR JOB: MAKE IT EASY

Let's say you've diagnosed the cause and the other person can complete the task, but it's really horrible and tedious. Now what? It's your job to help remove the barrier. It's your job to help make it easy. Unfortunately, not everyone agrees with this. In fact, some people take pride in their ability to inspire others to complete noxious or tedious tasks. In truth:

There is no great honor in being a leader or parent who is able to encourage people to continually achieve the nearly impossible. It can be gratifying to be an effective motivator, but the best leaders don't simply inspire people to continue to do the gut-wrenching, mind-boggling, and noxious. They help people find ways to ease the gut-wrenching, simplify the mind-boggling, and nullify the noxious.

This is where accountability experts truly shine. They see themselves as facilitators, enablers, and supporters, not armed guards or cheerleaders. This self-image may go further in separating the best from the rest than does any skill they actually possess.

Skilled individuals take pride in helping others make things easy. It's part of their Golden Rule. It's what they do.

Less skilled and more controlling folks have a different view of their role. They get people to do whatever it takes at whatever the cost and then brag about their leadership prowess. For them, making other people's burdens less burdensome is a sign of weakness. The home version of this attitude isn't any more attractive—for instance, getting your spouse to open up about a sensitive issue by piling on a truckload of guilt and manipulation. Why would anyone ever want to do such a thing? Because it's a power trip and some people love power more than they love relationships or even results.

Believing that it's praiseworthy to be able to compel people to complete tasks that are painful paints an intriguing yet counterintuitive picture of leadership. After all, human beings are forever finding ways to avoid pain and seek pleasure, not the other way around.

Distasteful tasks may be good for people at some level, and it's true that employees are generally getting paid to do them; but if they're normal human beings, they're going to try to find a way to get out of dreadful jobs or at least make them easier. Don't most of us use automatic garage door openers, punch TV remote-control buttons, and open cans with a special gadget of some kind? We don't *need* any of these things, but they make life easier.

It's important to make this distinction between necessity and convenience because we must be comfortable with the idea that it's okay for people to want to find an easier, more convenient way to do a job.

> Desiring to get out of hard and noxious work doesn't reflect a character flaw; it's what smart people do.

When your 12-year-old son goes to great pains to invent an automatic back scratcher or cons his friends into pushing him around the mall in a wheelchair, you can view him as either lazy or creative. And when someone who works for you runs into an ability barrier where the job is difficult but not impossible, you can apply your motivation tools to inspire him to keep his nose to the grindstone. Or you can find a way to make the task easier. Or you can do both.

For the remainder of this chapter, we're going to look at how to make it easy for others. We already know how to motivate. And we're going to take pride in the fact that we're making it easy. It's the smart thing to do.

TOOLS FOR MAKING IT EASY

Jointly Explore Barriers

Knowing *what* to do with an ability barrier is actually fairly simple: jointly explore the underlying ability blocks and remove them. That's easy. In contrast, knowing *how* to remove those barriers requires our attention. That means we need to know if others can't do something because of personal (they don't have the skills or knowledge), social (friends, family, or coworkers are withholding information or material), or structural (the world around them is structured poorly) factors. But before we consider the ability side of our Six-Source Model, we'll have to break years of bad habits.

Avoid Quick Advice

When we hear that someone faces an ability barrier, we habitually jump in with suggestions. We don't even think about it. We're experienced, and we understand how things work, and so when we see an ability challenge, we roll up our sleeves and fix things. It's positively Pavlovian. We see a problem, and *bing*, the gate is up and our tongues are off and running.

When people come to you and explain that they're at their wits' end, it's nearly guaranteed that you're going to tell them what to do. After all, they're asking you to tell them what to do. Nevertheless, jumping in with your answers isn't always the smart move.

Should You Do It Yourself?

Let's see how this problem plays itself out. A child brings you a broken toy, and you fix it, or at least you try. After all, the child either doesn't know what to do or doesn't have the skills or tools to do it, and so it's obvious that you need to do the work. It's the helpful thing to do. Or is it?

Resourceful people realize that when others face an ability block, you can either tell them outright what to do (if you know) or invite them to help come up with a solution: "What do you think it'll take to fix this?" "Would you like to help me?" Savvy folks choose to work jointly through ability blocks. They fight their natural tendency to jump in with an answer and instead involve the other person. Here's why.

Involvement Both Enables and Motivates

Enables

If you involve others in solving problems, two important things happen. First, you get to hear their ideas. People may not know exactly what to do, but they probably have a good idea about what *doesn't* work. Actually, they may know exactly what to do but need materials or permission to do it. In any case, start ability discussions with a simple question: "You've been working on the problem. What do you think needs to be done?" Ask them for their ideas. Invite them to put their theories, thoughts, and feelings on the table. They'll start to identify the barriers source by source.

When people aren't completely certain about what to do or if it becomes clear that they don't understand the situation fully, it's perfectly legitimate to chime in with what you think might help. Of course, *how* you toss in ideas makes a big difference. Style counts. The feeling of the conversation should be one of partnering. You're working together as intellectual equals, both of you throwing in your thoughts.

Motivates

There's an important secondary benefit to involving others. When people are included in coming up with a potential solution, they're more likely to be motivated to implement it, and that's important. Consider the following formula:

Effectiveness = accuracy × commitment

Most problems have multiple solutions. The effectiveness of a solution depends on the accuracy of the chosen tactic. That's obvious. It's equally important that the person implementing the tactic believe in it. That's where commitment comes into play.

A solution that is tactically inferior, but has the full commitment of those who implement it, may be more effective than one that is tactically superior but is resisted by those who have to make it work.

Let's be clear about what we're proposing. Many people argue that the reason for involving others is to trick them into thinking the ideas are their own so that they'll work harder to implement them. We're *not* suggesting that you manipulate people into thinking that your ideas are theirs. Involving others is not a cheap trick. We're simply proposing that other people do have ideas, that getting them out in the open is to everyone's advantage, and that when people are involved in the entire thought process, they see why things need to be done a certain way and are motivated to do it that way.

By involving others, you *empower* them. You provide them with both the means and the motive to overcome problems.

Start by Asking for Ideas

Involving people is better than merely telling people. But how should you do that? This is quite simple.

> Start by asking other people for their ideas. They're closest to the problem; start with their best thinking.

When we first trained people to deal with ability problems, it all seemed so simple. You ask others for their ideas, you get to hear their best thoughts, and they're empowered. What could be easier? Who could possibly mess this up? As it turns out, there are several ways to go wrong. Here are the top three tactics to avoid.

Don't Bias the Response

As we trained people with these materials over the years, many participants would try to involve the others in resolving an ability problem in the following way:

> *"So you haven't been able to get in touch with the lawyers. Here's an idea: drive over to their office and wait until they return. What do you think?"*

People who choose this tactic understand only half of the concept of empowerment. As long as they give the other person a chance to disagree, they feel okay.

Unfortunately, when you're speaking from a power base, offering up your idea first and then asking for the other person's approval misses the mark. You're likely to bias the other person. First, you're filling his or her head with your idea, and this can cut off new thinking. Second, you may inadvertently be sending the message that your idea is what you really want, and so others are not about to disagree with you.

In the example just mentioned, the person is likely to say, "Perfect, I'll drive across town."

Ask other people for their thoughts; wait for them to share their best ideas, and then, if it is still necessary, chime in with your thoughts. For example, when you are speaking to your teenage son about not clearing two feet of snow from your driveway, he explains that the gas-powered snow thrower is jammed.

You ask, "What will it take to fix it?" You have an idea but wait to hear what he has to say. He explains that he ran over the Sunday paper and the machine ate it, and now its throat is jammed. From there he explains what it'll take to clear it, what he's doing, and how long it'll take. You offer an idea about a better tool and a way to use it, and together you come up with a plan for what he'll do.

Don't Pretend to Involve Others

This mistake in involving other people in solving an ability barrier is propelled by two forces. First, you already have an idea and would prefer to implement it without involving others. Second, you believe that you now have to involve others because it's the politically correct thing to do. Here's what you come up with: you simply pretend to involve others by asking for their ideas, after which you subtly manipulate them to come around to your way of thinking.

As you might suspect, this technique comes off as glaringly manipulative. It looks more like sending a rat through a maze and periodically throwing it a pellet for making the correct turn than like engaging in a legitimate effort to involve another human being in removing an ability barrier. Here is an example:

> *"What do you think it'll take to get these things out on time?"* you ask.
>
> *"How about if we put more people on the job?"* (You grimace and shake your head.)
>
> *"I guess I could work overtime myself."* (This time you frown deeply.)
>
> *"I don't know. What if I leave out a few steps along the way?"*
>
> *"What did you have in mind?"* you inquire.
>
> *"We don't have to shrink-wrap the materials. That'll save a couple of hours."*
>
> *"No, not that. Maybe the paperwork."*
>
> *"I could leave out the billing until . . ."*
>
> *"I was thinking of different paperwork,"* you hint. *"How about the environmental reports?"*
>
> *"I love your idea. Delay the environmental stuff, and oh yeah, thanks for coming up with the perfect solution."*

People laugh when they watch a video of this script because this kind of thing happens all the time. Some parents practically have a doctorate in this technique:

> *"What would you like to have for dinner?"* Mom asks.
>
> *"Mac and cheese!"* the kids shout.
>
> *"I was thinking of something with more green in it."*
>
> *"Really old mac and cheese."*
>
> *"Funny. How about something with vegetables?"* Mom continues.
>
> *"Mac and cheese with green beans."*

"Nope," Mom says with a frown. *"Too starchy."* And the endless search for what Mom really has in mind continues.

The problem with these interactions is not that the person in authority had an opinion. These people do have opinions, and they're certainly allowed to share them or even give a unilateral command. That's not the problem. The problem comes when this person attempts to pass off his or her opinions as an involvement opportunity. The sham ends up looking like a game of "read my mind" and is quite insulting.

Involve others in solving ability blocks only if you're willing to listen to their suggestions.

Don't Feel the Need to Have All the Answers

This mistake is the product of low confidence and a bad idea. Newly appointed leaders are often unwilling to ask their direct reports for their thoughts because these leaders believe that if they don't appear to know everything about the job, they'll look incompetent. In their view, asking for ideas isn't a smart tactic; it's a sign of weakness. When they are facing an employee with an ability problem, the newly appointed do their best to share their insights. The last thing they want to do is query an employee who not only reports to them but obviously needs help.

Of all the bad ideas circulating the grapevine, pretending that leaders must know everything is among the most ridiculous and harmful. Leaders earn their keep, not by knowing everything, but by knowing how to bring together the right combination of people (most of whom know a great deal more about certain topics than the leader will ever know) and propel them toward common objectives.

Confident leaders are very comfortable saying, "It beats me. Does anyone know the answer to that?" or "I don't know, but I can find out."

A couple's version of not involving others takes an interesting turn. We're often unwilling to approach a loved one with a high-stakes problem until we've come up with the exact solution we want. The uncertainty of approaching a conversation without a bulletproof plan can be terrifying. What if we can't fix it all? What if there is no answer? What if our partner comes up with a really stupid answer? Thus, we think up everything in advance, precluding the other person's genuine involvement.

Completing the conversation in one's head—before one actually speaks—nullifies the whole purpose of an accountability discussion. The idea should be *jointly* to create *shared* solutions that serve your *Mutual* Purpose. If you feel compelled to prefabricate answers, consider this: you don't have to make it all better. All you have to do is collaborate. As you develop shared solutions, well-handled accountability discussions become the glue of your relationship; they help you face and conquer common enemies. Don't exclude your partner by developing a plan before you've even opened the conversation.

Parents struggle with the same issue. Should they hold true to the adage "Never let them see you sweat"? Obviously, kids need to know that adults are confident and in charge. They feel secure believing that grown-ups know what to do. So whatever you do, don't ask them for their ideas. It'll freak them out. Still, wouldn't it be better if children learned early on that their parents may be trying their best but don't always know everything?

Get over it. It's okay to ask children for their ideas. They will eventually (say, by age seven) know more than you do about all things electronic. Take comfort in the knowledge that you don't have to be omniscient or even "semiscient." You've been around. You bring home the bacon and cook it. You've been potty-trained for years. Don't worry. You already have enough power and credibility to guilt-trip your kids.

Look at the Six Sources of Influence

Let's assume that after observing someone who has failed to live up to a promise, you carefully diagnose the situation. It's clear that the other person is motivated but can't do what he or she has been asked. You stop, pause long enough to stifle your ingrained impulse to jump in with your best and smartest recommendation, and say, "You're closest to the problem. What do you think needs to be done?"

Having asked for the other person's view, it's time for us to return to our diagnostic tool. We need to think through jointly which of the potential sources is at play. We need to listen to the other person's recommendations and then do our best to partner with that person in thinking through the root causes.

This can be tricky. When it comes to *motivating* others, any single source can overcome all the detractors. You may hate doing your job, your friends may make fun of you for doing it, and your family may offer no support whatsoever, but you need the money. You're motivated. When it comes to motivation, one source is all it takes.

With ability, the opposite is true. Any single barrier can trump all the enabling forces. You know what to do and have the right materials to do it, but your coworker hasn't done his or her part. You're missing only one element, but you're dead in the water. When it comes to ability, since a single factor can stop all the other forces in the universe that have joined together to make it possible to do what's required, you'd better be good at exploring all possible detractors. Otherwise you could be minutes away from a severe disappointment. You, along with the other person, had better be good at exploring all the existing as well as all the potential ability barriers.

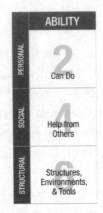

Brainstorm Ability Barriers

Let's assume that the other person is willing to look at the various forces that are making it hard to do what's required. But he or she is not completely aware of all the forces at play. The two of you will have to brainstorm the underlying causes. And if you want to do that, you need to be good at dealing with ability barriers that stem from personal, social, and structural factors.

Personal

Brainstorming personal ability issues can be tricky. As we suggested earlier, people often mask their inability. They'd rather point to other barriers than say they can't do something, particularly if the task is a basic part of the job. Make it safe for the other person to talk about personal challenges. Calmly ask about his or her comfort with doing the job, knowledge levels, and other skill factors. Keep the conversation upbeat.

Social

The enabling or disabling role others play is typically easier to discuss. This is about what other people are or are not doing, and so it can be less threatening. Nevertheless, when the people you're talking with worry about "ratting" on their colleagues, they may cover up for their friends by blaming other factors. Once again, make it safe to talk about colleagues and coworkers. Don't use a "find-the-guilty" tone. This isn't about blame or retribution; it's about finding and removing ability barriers.

Structural

The role the physical world plays in the problem is generally the easiest to discuss. People willingly point fingers at the things the company is doing to make their life more difficult—if they remember to think about them. Remember, human beings often forget the role of things in preventing them from achieving what they want to do. People also accept the physical world around them as a given, something that can't be changed: "Things have always been this way." Kick-start people's thinking. Ask about everything from systems, to work layout, to policies and procedures.

Three More Hints

As you jointly brainstorm ability barriers, don't forget to ask yourself the following three questions as the discussion winds down.

- *Will this person keep facing the problem?* When you are removing ability blocks, you must ensure that the problem won't keep resurfacing. Coming up with a one-time fix is hardly the preferred solution. For instance, the person doesn't have the materials needed. Making a phone call to secure the material solves the immediate problem but doesn't answer the question "Will this problem occur again, and why?"

- *Will others have similar problems?* This companion question explores the need for extending the solution to others. For example, a person doesn't know how to do the job. The two of you come up with a development plan. Will others need a similar plan, or is the problem unique to that person?

- *Have we identified all the root causes?* The ultimate question, of course, is "Have you brought to the surface all the forces, fixing them once and for all?" For instance, the person needs to take a software course. Why didn't the existing course help? The teacher was ineffective? Why was that? Japanese executives encourage leaders to ask why five times. We suggest that you probe until you've dealt with all the elements once and for all.

Advise Where Necessary

Our goal has been to collaborate with the other person in bringing to the surface and resolving ability blocks. We don't want to rush into solutions too quickly or force our ideas onto others. Besides, as we've argued all along, the people closest to a problem are likely to see more barriers than anyone else can. Nevertheless, there are times when people do need help. They can't see the barriers that have them stymied. In this case, it is our job to teach and advise, to point out stumbling blocks. In short, our job is to make invisible barriers more visible.

Think Physical Features

What kinds of barriers are most likely to remain a mystery to people? As we suggested earlier, most people have a hard time seeing organizational or environmental factors. The "things" around us are often static to the point of becoming invisible. Left to our own devices, we'd be the frog that boils to death in the pot because we miss the fact that the heat around us is increasing. We have a hard time noticing subtle forces such as the design of the environment, the availability of tools and technology, the chain of command, and policies and procedures.

For instance, your increasingly estranged relationship with your teenage son may be affected by the fact that he moved into the basement. Now the two of you bump into each other only in and around the vicinity of the refrigerator. Since you're on a diet and he no longer frequents the family room, you hardly see each other anymore. Be sure the natural flow of the physical world supports your social goals. Think "things." Help others see the impact of the physical world.

As far as work goes, it can be helpful to encourage people to identify the various bureaucratic forces that are preventing them from doing what needs to be done. With time and constant exposure, people start to accept rules, policies, and regulations as a given. They start treating them like commandments or laws of nature. Soon these highly constraining walls of bureaucracy become invisible.

Make them visible. Play the role of ignorant outsider. Keep asking, "Why can't we do that?" If a policy is no longer relevant, find a way to do away with it. If a rule is excessively constraining, secure permission to release the constraint. Every time someone passes a new company rule, you can bet it's in response to someone making a bad choice. Now everyone is restricted from ever making a choice:

"Listen up, folks. Roberta broke the law yesterday, so we'll all be going to jail."

Keep in mind that rules and policies don't solve everything and that the ones you make in-house you can unmake.

If you really want to help people identify hidden barriers, attack the paperwork. Look at forms and signatures as targets for change. If people can't complete their jobs on time because it takes seven signatures to get started, revisit why the signatures are required.

One company cut its response time in half by reviewing such a policy. The typical customer-service response couldn't begin until seven people signed off on a form. This was the liberating idea: Typically, three of the people needed to give approval, but the other four only needed to be informed. Allowing employees to act after three signatures and then routing the form to the other four after the fact rocked their world.

By all means give people easy access to the information they need to make the right choices. Make sure that from the mass of data that's out there, the right data are in front of the right people at the right time. For example, quit complaining that your daughter isn't following her diabetes regimen if she's cut off from the data (her various blood sugar levels and the consequences of each one) that would encourage her to do the right thing. You can harangue. You can beg. Or you can put numbers and charts in front of her.

Here's another helpful tool. To help surface all sources of influence, ask, "If you ran this place, what would you do to solve this problem?" Asking people to assume the role of the big boss can be extremely liberating. Freed from the shackles of thinking from within their own fields of influence, they begin to look for ways to remove every company-made barrier.

In short, think hidden forces, think lots of forces, and keep at it until you're satisfied that you've wrestled every single barrier to the ground.

CHECK BOTH SIDES

As you finish an accountability discussion, there's a danger that despite your efforts to surface all the causes behind an ability problem, you still have unfinished business. The person still might not be motivated. How could that happen? This typically occurs when you describe a problem and the person immediately identifies an ability barrier. People tend to point to an ability block because it's less threatening—even when they may also have conflicting priorities.

That brings us to our point. The fact that people start by identifying an ability block doesn't guarantee that once it's removed, they'll actually want to do what they've promised to do. Once you've finished identifying and removing ability barriers, check both sides of the model. Ask, "If I get the work-up to you by two o'clock, are you willing to do what it takes to finish the job by five, or is there something else I need to know?"

Checking both sides means that you end a discussion of ability by checking for motivation. Of course, it goes both ways. If a person starts with "Do you really want me to do that? It's such a pain," and you spend time explaining the natural consequences until he or she agrees to comply, there's a chance the person may also be facing an ability barrier or two. Once the person has agreed to comply, check the other side. Check for ability problems: "It sounds like you're willing to do this, but is there anything standing in your way? Is there anything else we need to deal with, or can I count on you having this to me by Tuesday at nine?"

Once you've dealt with motivation, check ability. If you start with ability, check motivation. Remember to check both sides.

Make It Safe for Others to Search

Let's end our discussion of ability problems by considering a difficult case. You want to brainstorm root causes with another person but don't have the authority to do so.

For instance, your boss promises to give you a hand with customers during peak hours, but he's routinely unavailable when you need him. Are you really going to have to motivate your boss to live up to his promise? Is that what's going on? One thing is certain: you want to get to the root cause. Does he dislike helping out because he doesn't like working with hostile customers? Does he think the work is beneath him? Are other priorities more important? Has he forgotten how to do the job?

You don't know what's actually going on here. Your only goal is to talk to your boss, identify the real forces behind his not helping, and learn if he's going to keep his commitment or if you're going to have to find a way to live without his help. That means you have to encourage your boss to join with you as you brainstorm reasons he isn't keeping his commitment. Or if you're in a real hurry, you could just step in front of a moving train.

Ask for Permission

We've talked about this before. If you lack the authority to require another person to discuss root causes, you can do so only by permission. So ask for it. If you do have the authority, ask for it anyway: "Since we agree on the problem, could we take a few minutes to talk about what's in the way of solving it? I'd like to be as helpful as I can in making it easy to avoid the problem in the future. Would that be okay?"

Ask for Feedback

Perhaps the most gracious way to open the door to a complete discussion of underlying causes is to ask if you are adding to the problem. When you take responsibility for your contribution, you make it safe for other people to do the same thing: "My goal is to solve the problem. I'm particularly interested in learning about anything I might be doing to contribute to the challenges you face."

Prime the Pump

People often feel unsafe discussing root causes because they fear that any analysis will make them look weak or selfish. If they're not able, that's bad. If they're not motivated, that may look worse. You need to change this view. Your job in leading a root-cause discussion is to let others know that you see them as people of worth who are currently unable to do what's expected. This isn't about fixing their character; it's about a fixing a problem.

One of the best ways to assure others that you're not going to get angry when you learn the root cause is to "prime the pump," or take your best guess at possible causes, without looking stressed, miffed, or judgmental. This helps others start the flow of information by making it safe for them to speak honestly. Priming works only if you take your best guess in a way that tells the other person that you're okay with him or her admitting to what you just described. Word choice, body language, and tone of voice make a huge difference. Consider the following question: "Is that too hard for you?"

Now read the line in a patronizing way. Next, do it in anger. To draw on your real talents, read the line with sarcasm.

Finally, try to be respectful. Imagine that this is a person you care about and genuinely want to help. How does that affect your delivery?

When priming is done well, it provides others with real-time visible evidence that you're not going to demean or criticize them for honestly discussing the real issues. In short, your success depends on whether you see other people as human beings or villains. If you've come to see others as people you want to help succeed, most of the time you'll do just fine.

CHAPTER SUMMARY

Make It Easy

We've carefully described the gap and are now listening to see if the problem is due to motivation or ability. In this chapter, we examined the ability side of the model. When the other person isn't able, it's our job to make it easy.

- When facing ability barriers, make impossible tasks possible and nasty tasks less nasty. In short, when others face ability barriers, make it easy.

- Jointly explore root causes. Take care to avoid jumping in with your own solutions. Empower others by allowing them to take part in diagnosing the real cause and coming up with workable solutions. Ask others for their ideas. Remember the all important question "What do you think it'll take?"

- When others can't identify all the causes, jointly explore the underlying forces—include personal, social, and structural factors. Remember the model. When necessary, stimulate the brainstorming process by including your own view of what some of the barriers may be.

- Once you're finished with surfacing and resolving ability barriers, check both sides. See if others are willing to do what's required once you've taken steps to enable them. Just because they can do something, doesn't mean they're willing.

What's Next?

Now it's time to move on to the next problem. What happens if you're in the middle of an accountability discussion and a whole new infraction emerges? Do you dare deal with it? Do you dare not? How can you stay both focused and flexible?

6

Stay Focused and Flexible

What to Do When Others Get Sidetracked, Scream, or Sulk

Up to this point we've created a map showing how to master an accountability discussion. It's intended to describe key principles and skills, not fixed roads laid down on an unmovable terrain. This means that the principles and skills have to be woven into a workable script on the spot, as the conversation unfolds.

This on-the-spot creativity calls for an enormous amount of flexibility. After we describe the gap, we have to diagnose what's happening. Are people failing to come through because of a motivation problem, or is it ability? Otherwise, we're likely to charge in blindly and apply the wrong prefabricated fix: "I can't believe that you came to our biggest meeting of the year a full 30 minutes late. . . . Oh, your mom's funeral, huh?"

That was awkward.

It gets worse. Not only do we have to work unrehearsed and on the fly, but we have to be flexible enough to deal with new problems as they seem to appear out of nowhere. You're talking about problem X, and problem Y emerges right there on the spot.

For instance, you're talking to a coworker about doing his fair share of the workload, and he becomes angry. You're chatting with your daughter about failing to practice the piano, and she lies to you. You're talking to an employee about missing a deadline, and he becomes insubordinate. You're talking to your unemployed husband about actively looking for work, and he tries to divert you from the problem by playing the martyr. Your head accountant clams up when you ask her why the end-of-month reports aren't ready. Then she gets angry. All these situations present you with new, emergent problems.

WE MUST BE FOCUSED AND FLEXIBLE

As new problems emerge, we have to be focused enough not to get sidetracked. We can't let every breeze blow us in a different direction. By the same token, we have to be flexible enough to step away from the current issue and deal with the new problems on the spot if necessary.

When a brand-new problem with a life of its own comes up in the middle of an accountability discussion, we have to make a decision. Do we step away from the current infraction (putting a bookmark in place so that we can get back to it later) and address the new problem? Or do we stay the course? This takes us back to the issue we addressed in Chapter 1: What is the right conversation? Now we're introducing the idea that the right conversation can change before your eyes.

The answer to this new *if* question is simple. If the new, emergent problem is more serious, time sensitive, or emotional than the original one or if it's important to the other person, you have to deal with it right there, on the spot. You can't allow the new and more important issue to be at the mercy of the original violation.

For example, you can't have your daughter lying to you. Lying is worse than missing practice. You can't allow an employee to become insubordinate. If you don't say something right away, you undermine your credibility. You can't allow a person to fume and boil and pretend nothing is happening. It'll only get worse.

The good news is that if you choose to move to the new and emergent topic, all the skills we've looked at so far are applicable. Of course, if you decide to deal with the new problem, you need to do so in a focused way. Don't be tricked into getting sidetracked and don't drift aimlessly from topic to topic. Carefully transition when you change your focus. In short, as new and emergent problems surface, do the following:

- *Be flexible:*
  - Note new problems.
  - Select the right problem: the original problem, the new one, or both.
  - Resolve the new problem and return to the original issue.

- *Be focused:*
  - Deal with problems one at a time.
  - Consciously choose to deal with new issues; don't allow them to be forced upon you.

FOUR DIFFERENT EMERGENT PROBLEMS AND HOW TO ADDRESS THEM

To see how this works, let's look at four different categories of new problems: there is a loss of safety, there is a loss of trust, a completely different issue becomes a problem, and explosive emotions take over. Each category requires the same basic skills, but each is different enough that it deserves careful and separate attention.

People Feel Unsafe

This is the most common emergent problem, and we talked about it earlier. You're discussing a failed promise, and the other person becomes frightened and starts to pull away from the discussion or push too hard. Either response brings a healthy conversation to a screeching halt. Fear, and the resulting silence or violence, is the emergent problem.

If you don't step out of the existing conversation and establish safety, you're never going to resolve the issue at hand. So that's what you do. You step out, create safety, and step back in. In this case you don't need to acknowledge a change in topic because you aren't changing topics. You're simply dealing with the real problem, which is not the topic itself but the fact that the other person feels unsafe discussing it.

To restore safety, you point to your shared purpose. You assure the other person that you care about what he or she cares about. You use Contrasting to clarify the misunderstanding. You apologize when necessary. You make it safe. If you don't, you'll never be able to resolve the original issue.

For example, you're talking to a coworker about not helping you out on a boring job. She agreed to lend a hand, but she took a phone call and then disappeared until you finished the noxious task. You describe the problem, tentatively sharing your path. You wonder if she purposely left and didn't return until she knew that the dreadful job had been done. She immediately becomes offended, averts her eyes, and says in a hurt tone, "Are you saying I'm not a good friend? That I take advantage of you? Is that what you think of me?"

You respond by sharing your common purpose: "I was just hoping to come up with a way to ensure that we're both working on the job we hate the most. Neither of us likes to do it." Then you Contrast: "I didn't mean to imply that you weren't a good friend. I think you are. I just wanted to talk about the one job." Then you apologize: "I'm sorry if it sounded like I was falsely accusing you. I'm just curious about why you left in the middle of a job when you knew I really wanted you to lend a hand."

People Violate Your Trust

This is probably the most dangerous emergent problem, the number one killer of accountability, and the chief reason most people can't hold others accountable without breaking out in hives. You ask a person who reports to you why he failed to attend the computer training class he had agreed to sit in on, and he explains that he would have been there but "something came up."

Not knowing if this is code for a motivation problem or an ability problem, you ask him exactly what prevented him from keeping his promise. You're thinking that if it wasn't a meteorite crashing into his cubicle, you're not going to be all that sympathetic. You know he hates computer training. However, he desperately needs it, and so you inconvenienced everyone else on the work team to schedule it around his needs. Now he's telling you that something came up:

> "*Omar in payroll needed someone to run over to head-quarters for him, and I was the only one who drove to work today. Everyone else came in on the subway.*"
> "*And running an errand for Omar was more important than the training?*" you ask.
> "*Of course! It was the payroll.*"
> "*Well, yes, the payroll is important.*"

The problem with what just happened is that you allowed this to become a conversation about choosing payroll over training. That's not the big issue, at least not yet. It should be a conversation about trust. The other person made a promise and unilaterally decided to break it. This is a huge violation of trust and an insult to the relationship. To mask this breach of accountability, the other person focuses on the content (payroll versus training) rather than the relationship.

Is this a big deal? Almost nothing in a company, including the payroll, is more important than finding a way to fix the lack of accountability this scene depicts. The person failed to live up to a commitment, and nothing happened. Actually, he was allowed to ignore the real issue: the broken promise.

Something Came Up

Companies that continually allow things to come up without dealing with the breach of promise don't survive very long. And while they are limping along, they're horrible places to work. Nothing destroys trust more than casually giving assignments and then hoping against hope that people will deliver. You may like the fact that your boss doesn't always follow up with you, giving you substantial freedom, but you hate it when others are equally loose and unpredictable. Heaven help the company that lets things come up.

In a similar vein, when family members allow one another to break promises and ignore the consequences, pain and suffering are just around the corner. When it comes to child rearing, arbitrary accountability is a big contributor to delinquency and insecurity. Giving family members the luxury of arbitrarily choosing which promises they'll keep—turning life into a cafeteria of commitments in which people can keep one of this one but not one of those—drives people insane.

The Intersection of Flexibility and Focus

Let's be realistic. Things do come up. In today's tumultuous world, changes occur all the time, and if you can't make mid-course corrections as new information pours in, your company will die. You have to be strong and flexible. You have to be able to bend but not break.

How can you be at once focused and flexible? It's actually easy. At the heart of every workable accountability system, there is one simple sentence: "If something comes up, let me know as soon as you can."

This sentence represents the marriage of flexibility and focus. In these 12 words, two seemingly contradictory elements form a perfect harmony: the yin and yang of accountability. Although the words are sparse, to speak them is to say:

> *"I want you to live up to your promise. Please don't unilaterally break it. I want you to focus on getting the job done. At the same time, I realize that the world can change. Things come up. Many of these barriers will negate your existing promise. If something does come up, let me know as soon as possible so there are no surprises and so we can decide together how to handle the situation."*

Consider the following situations:

Sometimes the thing that comes up will affect motivation. For example, your son is on the way to take a makeup algebra test after school and his uncle stops him along the route and asks him to go to the movies. He's been lonely since his divorce, and your son thinks he should go along. So he wants to change his priority. But not without talking to you. Together you should decide if your son should provide familial support or if he should take the makeup test, or maybe you can find a way to do both.

Sometimes the thing that comes up will affect ability. For instance, the air-conditioning unit breaks down, and the production manager thinks she should let everyone go home early even though she promised to finish a project. This may be the right solution, but she should first check with the major stakeholders (in this case, her boss) to see if this is the best solution for the situation. Maybe, based on the reasons for the deadline and the costs of missing it, it makes better business sense to pay the service experts overtime plus a surcharge to get the equipment fixed right away.

With a policy of "If something comes up, let me know as soon as you can," we should expect pretty immediate communication. Thanks to modern technology, when we say, *"Let's talk as soon as you can,"* we know that can be pretty fast. Between e-mail, voice mail, text messages, and cell phones, we are always no farther away from each other than the speed of light and the click of a button. To put this in perspective, you can track someone down in China about a hundred million times faster than Marco Polo.

The Foundation of Crucial Accountability

Let's return to our friend who told us that he didn't attend the computer class because something came up. What should we say to him? Naturally, the way we approach the failed promise will depend on our own private history of accountability. If our company promises are merely rough guidelines, include the possibility of a surprise, or are made with a wink, we've reaped what we've sown. There's really not much we can say. In fact, in a huge number of companies (and families are no different), the following is true:

Results = no results + a good story

In institutions where accountability is shaky, people treat you as if you've succeeded as long as you have a good excuse or story. In this inventive culture, failure accompanied by a plausible excuse equals success. And we all know what the good story is: "Something came up." It's the catchall story. It keeps you from ever being held accountable—that is, if friends, family, bosses, and coworkers actually let you get away with it.

But you know better. You understand that an accountability discussion by definition deals with broken commitments, and if you don't have to keep commitments, everything falls apart. You also know that things change, and so if there is a need to change, talk as soon as you can.

Therefore, when you first started working with your team, you spoke in great detail about the all-important sentence: "If something comes up, let me know as soon as you can."

You explained how these few words, when honored, bring predictability into a turbulent world. You spoke eloquently about how this simple phrase emphasizes the importance of both the need for flexibility and the need for predictability. You talked about how it forms the very foundation of trust. And finally, when you first talked with your direct report about attending the computer class, you ended by reaffirming your stance. You said, "By the way, if something comes up, let me know as soon as you can." And you meant it.

So what do you say to the fellow who thinks that as long as Omar in payroll asked him to do something important, he has been liberated from his original promise? What is the right conversation to have? The problem isn't that he didn't attend the class (that is *a* problem but not *the* problem); the problem is that he saw what he thought called for a change in the plan and changed it. Not only did he make the choice on his own, but he didn't have the courtesy to call you. He left you completely out of the decision. That's a trust problem.

Guess what: if you talk about the training issue and not about the trust problem, you'll walk away dissatisfied and trusting the person even less, and you won't even realize that you've had the wrong conversation. Of course, if you do talk about mistrust, the consequences of violating one's word must be severe.

You no longer know if the other person will honor his word. Predictability is shaky. You may have to monitor him more closely. You may have to follow up more frequently. You don't want to do this, and he's not going to like it. This is the new problem, and these are some of the attendant consequences.

> ### Create a Bedrock of Trust
>
> To establish a climate in which accountability discussions are built on a bedrock of trust, stay focused. Set clear and firm expectations. Stay flexible. End by stating, "If something comes up, let me know as soon as you can." Finally, when you're talking with someone who tries to excuse a missed assignment by saying that "something came up," deal with this emergent problem—this violation of trust—as a new challenge. Never let it slide.

New Problems Sneak onto the Scene

Let's look at another category of emergent problems. You're talking about a failed expectation, and the other person, besides saying that something came up, does something that is actually worse than the original infraction.

For instance, you're the only female member of your team at work. You're talking to a coworker who somehow always seems to find a way to get out of the tasks nobody likes to do. You've agreed to share all jobs equally, there are four of you, and he works on the disagreeable assignments only about 10 percent of the time. This math isn't working for you.

You decide to talk about your conclusion that he's purposely skipping out of the unpopular jobs, knowing that you'll start with the facts and then tentatively tell him what you and others are beginning to conclude. This actually goes fairly well. Then he says, "You know, I'm glad you brought up the issue. Women shouldn't let guys like me walk all over them. In fact, I like women who are strong."

You continue along the problem-solving path, trying to see if he'll agree to take his fair share of the noxious tasks, and he adds, "Forceful women are a bit of a turn-on."

He's now leaning close to you and sort of leering. You don't like leaning and leering, and you really don't like the words *turn on* unless they refer to an electrical switch. So you tell him that, including the semifunny electrical switch line. You figure you'll use humor to break the tension.

He comes back with "Exactly what *are* your turn-ons?"

Okay, that's it. Given his insensitive persistence, you decide to step away from the fairness issue and confront the new problem. He is acting inappropriately, and you don't like it. In fact, it feels like harassment. This is the problem you want to discuss. The behaviors, of course, include using sexual innuendo, leaning, and leering.

To deal with this tricky emergent problem, start by announcing the change in topic. It's okay to change topics, but always clarify what you're doing. Place a bookmark where you just were so that it will be easy to return to it later. If you don't, you lose your place and sometimes forget that you changed topics: "I'd like to talk about what just happened."

This stops the conversation dead in its tracks. Next, do everything you've learned so far. Pick the problem you want to discuss. Take charge of your harsh feelings by telling a story other than "He's a filthy pig who needs to die a painful death." What's likely to be going on is that he thinks he's flirting and it's cute. He actually believes that. Bring your emotions under control by telling a more accurate story. Then describe the gap. Move from the content conversation to the relationship one (his disrespectful behavior): "You just made references to your 'turn-ons,' you moved so close to me that I felt uncomfortable, and your eyes were moving up and down my body. What's going on here?"

Shocked that anyone would actually call him on something he's been getting away with for years, he apologizes and says it won't happen again.

You then close the discussion by seeking a clear commitment: "So I can count on you to treat me like a professional in the future?"

He quickly nods in agreement.

That was easy. No need for consequences. No need to analyze underlying ability blocks: "Sorry, I was raised by wild animals and am a bit of a social moron." He agrees to back off, and your life just got better.

Now you face one more issue. Do you return to the original problem? You still haven't resolved the job equity issue. This is something you have to decide in the moment. Sometimes, having dealt with a much larger problem, you decide to return to the original problem another time. Continuing now could seem like piling it on. Besides, in this case he may want to make a hasty exit to regain his dignity and composure. Naturally, if there is enough safety to continue, go ahead and finish what you started. Retrieve the bookmark and continue where you left off.

> These steps can be applied to any new problem that emerges in the middle of an accountability discussion. Pull out of the original infraction, announce the change in topic, discuss the new infraction, bring it to a satisfactory resolution, and then decide whether you need to return to the original issue.

For instance, you're talking to your seven-year-old daughter about not practicing the piano as she promised she would. She explains that she did practice. You were sitting at the piano folding clothes during the appointed time, and so you tell her that and end with "Since you weren't here, how did you practice?" Your daughter bursts into tears because she's been caught in a lie. You now have a new and bigger problem.

"I didn't practice because I hate practicing at four o'clock every day," she says. "That's the best playtime, and I miss being with my friends."

Now you know why she didn't practice, but that's no longer the problem you want to discuss. She lied. This is now a relationship conversation. Of course, she wants to talk about the inconvenient practice time (the content issue). That solves her problem. It also takes the focus off the bigger issue: she lied. Make sure to have the right conversation:

> *"I'd like to talk about what just happened."*
> *"What's that?"*
> *"When I asked you about your piano practice, you said that you did practice, but you didn't."*
> *"That's because everyone plays kickball in the cul-de-sac, and I love to play kickball."*
> *"What I'd like to talk about is not your practice time; we'll get back to that later.* [Place a bookmark.] *I want to talk about the fact that you lied to me."* [Announce the new topic.]

Then you talk about lying. She says she'll never ever do it again, but you fear that she doesn't fully understand the consequence of her lying, and so you choose to explain what happens when you can no longer take her at her word. You treat this as a teaching moment, explain the natural consequences that result from lying, and work through the problem, and she apologizes. Then she wants to get back to the trouble with her piano practice time, which you resolve by moving it to a later hour.

Pull out, announce the change in topic, confront the new problem, work it through to a satisfactory resolution, and then decide whether you want to return to the original infraction. Of course, this can work only if you spot the new problem and then choose to deal with it. This can be difficult when you're already trying to handle another problem, but that's how the world of human interaction unfolds. New problems emerge all the time.

Sometimes you can experience three different emergent problems in a couple of minutes, and you have to decide which ones to confront. For instance, you're talking with your husband, who is out of work and isn't spending much time seeking employment. You make enough to support the two of you, and he's starting to look far too comfortable staying at home and surfing the net. You're from the school of thought that says that if you lose your old job, your new job is finding a job, and so you step up to that accountability conversation.

Your husband responds by saying that it's not his fault that the economy is so horrible. Then he starts playing on your emotions by explaining how awful he feels and saying that you should be more sympathetic to him because offshore workers have ruined his career.

When your husband was first laid off, he didn't do much to find a new job, and so you jointly developed a plan in which he agreed to work at getting work. That included eight hours a day of looking, sending out résumés, filling out applications, and so forth. He's not doing it, and that's the broken promise you want to talk about. He obviously wants to talk about a whole lot of other things, not his broken promise. You step back to the original problem by returning to the notion that he's supposed to be working at getting a job: That's the gap you describe. Now he calls you a nag and asks you to get off his back.

At this point you have several issues you may want to address. To help select the right problem, let's return to our CPR model. First, there's the *content*: Is he going to look for work? That's the original problem, and it's a big deal to you. You're not going to be easily sidetracked. Second, there's the *pattern*: This is the third time you've had to bring up the issue. Third, there are several *relationship* issues: He's playing with your emotions by asking for sympathy instead of talking about the violated promise.

He's trying to sidetrack you, and that feels manipulative. He's labeling you as a nag and taking the focus off the original problem, and this feels insulting.

To help you choose from the CPR model which combination of these issues to deal with, you can apply the questions we asked in Chapter 1. When the turf is changing with each paragraph, it's probably easiest to ask yourself, "What is it that I really want?" This will help you decide which issues to address.

Explosive Emotions Take Over

Now let's take emergent problems to the final level. The other person goes to silence or violence and becomes quite emotional. This person isn't merely pushing his or her argument too hard; he or she is becoming angry and abusive. Now what? You can't use the standard methods for creating safety until the other person has calmed down. Let's look at an example.

Going "Posthole"

You work as a manager for a small family-owned company that imports gardening implements from the Far East. You notice that Carl, a rather large, gruff fellow who works as your accountant, hasn't finished a month-end report that you asked to have by the end of yesterday. You walk into Carl's office and start an accountability discussion.

To make sure you don't set a bad tone, you describe the gap: "Carl, I noticed that the monthly report wasn't in my box this morning. Did you run into a problem?" Carl explains that he didn't know that it really mattered; besides, he really hates doing it. You don't leap to your power. Instead, you share a couple of natural consequences. Carl then states that he'll get right on it. No big deal.

That's how you expect the interaction to unfold. You act professionally, and your efforts pay off. However, there are exceptions. For instance, you carefully describe the problem, but Carl hasn't read this book. Despite the fact that you have been the picture of professionalism, he becomes angry and says: "I'm your best employee, I miss one deadline, and you're all over me. Leave me alone!"

Then he grabs a sales sample, a half-size posthole digger (one of your gardening products), and throws it at a file cabinet. Now what do you do?

What Is This Thing Called Anger?

To deal with a person who becomes emotional (this includes anger, frustration, fear, sorrow, etc.), we have to get to the source of all feelings. Let's return to the Path to Action.

Once again, emotions don't come from outer space. We create them ourselves. A person violates an expectation, we see it, and then we tell ourselves a story. The story then leads to a feeling.

To create a *strong* feeling, we tell a story that includes a strong value. For instance, a coworker lets you down on purpose. She disrespects you. Your boss double-checked your work because he doesn't trust you. Jordan got the raise because the policy is unfair. Your neighbor drove too fast because she doesn't care about your safety. These are sacred values. You become quite upset. Then, of course, your adrenaline kicks in, and it's off to the world of strong feelings, weak mind.

We become righteously indignant only when others have tread on sacred ground.

If you want to deal with your own emotions, you have to deal with your own stories. You have to find a way to tell them differently, leading to a different feeling and different actions. But how do you deal with *other people's* emotions? How do you affect *their* stories?

Take Carl. You ask him about a simple report, and he goes "posthole." He's one of your most level-headed employees. Obviously, there's more going on here than meets the eye. Despite the fact that you started the conversation with a professional description of the problem, he wiggled out of it. He raised his voice, told you to leave him alone, and tossed an object at a file cabinet. Although you may not know exactly what to do, you figure that his hurling a sharp object can't be a good sign.

You do know some things. First, Carl isn't simply responding to your opening question. You're picking up the conversation in the middle of a lengthy argument Carl has been making to himself. Second, Carl is not in a position to talk about the issue calmly and rationally. He's feeling the effects of adrenaline. Third, to diffuse the anger you'll have to get at Carl's underlying story, and he's the one who made it up, not you.

Dealing with Anger

First, Ensure Your Safety

Fortunately, Carl gave you the corporate, not the Neanderthal, version of a fight. He held thousands of years of genetic engineering in check by not attacking you. Then again, he did throw something at an innocent file cabinet. You figure that he was putting on a show and not out of control. You don't believe that you're in danger.

That is exactly what you should be determining. When other people become angry, there is always the chance that they will become violent. They've stepped over one line. Will they step over the next one? Fortunately, most bosses never face anything close to this form of danger at work, at least not from employees. People go to silence more than they go to violence. They complain to their loved ones. They play the martyr and despise you. They carp and seethe, but they don't explode.

Nevertheless, there are exceptions. That's why you must determine how dangerous the situation is. No listening skill or anger-reduction technique will overcome a person who is chasing you around the desk with a letter opener.

Don't be a hero. If you think you're in danger, leave. Remove yourself from the situation. Take flight; don't fight. Then call the appropriate authorities. In most companies that's security or human resources. Let your boss know what happened. Don't even think about dealing with the danger yourself.

Second, Dissipate the Emotion

If you're not in danger, go straight to the emotion; don't deal with the argument per se. If someone came to you strung out on drugs, you wouldn't dream of talking to that person about a work-related problem without first dealing with the chemical influence. It's ludicrous to assume that you can have a rational argument with a person who is under the influence of mood-altering stimuli.

Anger creates a similarly inflated and abnormal reaction. Anger-based chemicals are legal, of course, but they prepare the body to spring into action, and that doesn't mean talking politely. Therefore, don't deal with the content of the argument until you've dealt with the emotion. The other person isn't very likely to listen to you—or, for that matter, explain his or her own argument clearly and calmly—until the chemical surge has subsided. Any argument you make won't be heard. Any suggestions you offer are likely to come across as an assault. Stifle your desire to jump into the content of the argument. Instead, dissipate the emotion.

But how? What does it take to douse internal fires that have been fueled by unhealthy stories?

Common but Not Good Practices
Dealing with anger nose to nose, so to speak, is tremendously hard, so hard that it's almost impossible to find someone who does a good job of it. Here are three things not to do:

1. *Don't get hooked.* Left to our natural tendencies, most of us respond to anger in kind. We get hooked. We become the very monsters we're facing. But then again, why should we expect anything else? Someone who believes that a core value has been violated becomes angry. He or she hurls that anger in our faces, violating one or more of our core values. We become angry in response.

2. *Don't one up.* It's hard to imagine that anyone would treat anger with smug indifference, but it happens:

   An employee barks, *"That's the third time in a row accounting has screwed up my check!"*

   The boss strikes back with *"Big deal. When I held your job, I had to walk six blocks to pick up my pay. There was a time when I didn't get a red cent for almost two months, and that was over Christmas no less! You've got it easy."*

   When other people become angry, they want first to talk about and then to resolve their problem, not yours. They certainly don't want to be told that their problem can't compete with your lengthy and impressive history of disappointments and disasters.

3. *Don't patronize.* Acting holier than thou *really* doesn't work, as this example shows:

   One of your direct reports charges into your office and complains, *"What was Larry trying to do in that meeting? He humiliated me in front of everyone!"*

You come back with *"Now, now. Quit throwing a child-ish tantrum. If you expect to talk to me, you'll need to act like an adult."* Or you might say, *"I can see you're out of control. Here's some money. Go get a cup of coffee and return when you're under control."*

Telling people to calm down or grow up throws gas on the flames of violated values. They're already fuming about being mistreated, and then you heap on more abuse. You patronize them. Your tone tells them that you think you're superior. And as if this isn't bad enough, you act as if you're their confidant, giving them helpful advice.

Third, Explore the Other Person's Path to Action

To see what we should do in the face of strong emotions, let's return to our Path to Action.

Try to See More Than the Action

When someone becomes noticeably emotional, we see only the action that comes out at the end of their path. In fact, all we can ever see is anyone's action or behavior. Everything else—feelings, stories, and observations—gets trapped inside.

Get to the Source

Because we can never see what's going on inside other people's heads, it's important to help bring their thoughts and feelings into the open. This requires some skill on our part. We've seen the action; now it's our job to retrace their Path to Action to whatever it was that ticked them off. We must move from the emotional outburst back to the feeling, the story, and the original observation. Therein lies the source of the emotion as well as the solution to the problem.

Use AMPP to Power Up Your Listening Skills

Next, we have to find a way to understand why others get emotional as well as let them know that we understand. We have four power listening tools to help us. We'll use the acronym AMPP to help us recall them and as a reminder that they boost the power of our pathfinding skills. For those of you who are familiar with our previous book, *Crucial Conversations: Tools for Talking When Stakes Are High*, this material should have a familiar ring.

AMPP reminds us that we can simply *ask* to get the conversation rolling, *mirror* to encourage, *paraphrase* for understanding, and *prime* to make it safe for the other person to open up.

Ask to Get Things Rolling

Sometimes others convey their strong emotions but say little or nothing about what's going on. You can tell that they're frustrated or upset or even angry, but they're not opening up. For instance, your teenage son walks into the house, slams the door, and throws his books on the kitchen table. He looks pretty upset to you, but he doesn't say a word. You start with a simple probe:

"What's going on?"

He comes back with the classic "Nothin'!"

You ask him to join in a conversation: "No, really. I'd love to hear what happened."

"I don't want to talk about it."

Maybe he really doesn't want to talk. Maybe he does but has to be encouraged a little. He wants to know that you care enough to stick with it. The trouble is that both conditions start with the same signal: "I don't want to talk about it."

You ask him one more time by saying: "Honest, I'm all ears. I promise I'll just listen. Sometimes that can help."

"Well, this morning before science class . . ."

Mirror to Encourage

When you're talking to emotionally charged people, you may want to do more than simply ask them to talk. You may want to bring in a bigger gun: mirroring.

Here's how it works. Say Tom, one of your direct reports, sat glumly in a meeting, said nothing, and looked discouraged. Normally Tom is upbeat and contributes a lot to meetings. As the meeting ends, you find yourself alone with Tom, and so you start with a simple probe: "Are you feeling okay?"

In truth, he's not. He's upset and a little embarrassed. Over the last year Tom has put on 30 pounds, and people have taken to calling him "big guy." You started the meeting by praising the "big guy" for his recent accomplishments. Your praise, wrapped in the negative label, hurt Tom's feelings. However, when you ask him, he's reluctant to say anything. After all, you are the boss and it's sort of embarrassing. So he comes back with "Well, uh, I'm, uh . . . I'm feeling just fine."

Only he says it in a tone of voice and with a body posture that communicate exactly the opposite. To encourage Tom to open up, you hold a mirror up to him; that is, you describe the inconsistency between what he just said and how he just said it: "You know, the way you said that makes me wonder if you are okay. You seem kind of, I don't know, low-energy, maybe a bit glum. Are you sure you're okay?"

What you're trying to do, of course, is make it safe for Tom to talk. By holding up a mirror, you're letting him know that you're concerned and that his brush-off wasn't taken at face value. Once again, you're trying to open up a conversation, not compel Tom to spill his guts.

Paraphrase for Understanding

Sometimes you catch a break. Say an employee is upset, walks in, and dumps out her entire Path to Action in one fell swoop: "Boy, am I miffed. You can be so controlling. It drives me crazy. Yesterday I got another one of your follow-up notes. Do you have to monitor me by the hour? I feel like I'm being baby-sat!"

She has shared her feeling (miffed), her story (you control me too much because you don't trust me: the violated value), and the fact that her feeling is based on either the note you sent her or your history of sending notes to check on how things are going.

With this much information on the table, it's best to check to see if you understand what she said. Paraphrase; that is, put in your own words what you think she stated. But don't parrot. Restating *exactly* what the other person said can be annoying and often sounds phony. Simply take your best guess at what the person just expressed:

"You're upset because you think I overmanage you? I'm too controlling and send you too many notes—is that it?"

Paraphrasing serves two functions. First, it shows that you are listening and that you care. This alone often calms the other person down enough to allow a rational conversation. Second, it helps you see what you do and don't understand.

"No, I don't care about the notes," she says. "It bugs me that you give me more notes than anyone else. Do you really think I'm the least competent person here?"

Ah, so it's an issue of equity or respect (different core values).

"You think I give you more notes than others, that I don't respect you?"

"Well, yeah. Yesterday you talked to Ken and then let him go without so much as a single follow-up. But with me. . . ."

Prime to Make It Safe

Sometimes it takes quite a bit to encourage other people to talk openly. They figure that speaking their minds is a bad idea. If they express their feelings openly, they're likely to get into trouble.

You've invited and mirrored, but so far the other person has remained emotionally charged *and* mute. What next? Our final tool takes us right into the other person's story. We prime: we add words to the conversation (much like putting water in a pump to get it flowing), hoping the other person will do the same thing. We do this by guessing what the other person may be thinking: "Are you upset because I did something unfair? I gave the promotion to Margie, and maybe you think that you're more qualified or that I didn't do a good job of making a choice. Is that it?"

The second half of this skill lies in *how* you guess the story. You're trying to make it safe for others to share their thoughts. That means you have to express your best guess in a way that says, "Don't worry; I'll be okay with this discussion. I won't become defensive or angry." You do this, of course, by stating the story calmly and matter-of-factly.

Fourth, Take Action

Openly talking about the other person's path puts us in a position to deal calmly with the issues that have surfaced. If we willingly talk about people's thoughts and feelings without mocking, squelching, or attacking them, they are much more likely to calm down enough to both express their thoughts and listen to ours. Once we've uncovered the story and the action that led to it, we're in a position to deal with the problem itself, and this is what we should do. We're not listening for the sake of listening. Once again, we're learning about how to carry on an accountability discussion, in this case how to listen actively not as an intellectual exercise but as a way to get to results.

Create a Safety Valve

Before we bring this chapter to a close, let's look at one final issue. You approach your boss with a problem that he is causing, and he immediately becomes aggressive. You silently seethe because you were hoping he would help you resolve the problem, not shoot the messenger. Despite your best efforts to stifle the fuming volcano of hate and loathing that is overtaking your "employee of the month" persona (which at the awards banquet just last month won you a free week's dry cleaning), your boss picks up on your hostile tone and warns you that you're starting to "step across the line."

You find his remarks duplicitous because his tone is always snippy and insulting, but in a thinly veiled sarcastic kind of way that he thinks is clever and you think places him in the top five in the pantheon of hypocrites. You're at a crossroads. To paraphrase Woody Allen, one path leads to despair and utter hopelessness; the other, to total extinction. You can only pray that you have the wisdom to choose correctly.

Actually, you have a third choice. You can step back and buy yourself time. You can and should take a strategic delay: "You know what; I need to think about this in more detail. I'll get back to you later."

And with that short comment, you hotfoot it back to your office. This is not a retreat. It's a strategic delay. This is not silence; you plan on returning. Once you're ensconced in the safety of your office, you take a deep breath, regain control of your emotions, think about a new and better strategy for talking about the problem, and return another hour or day.

If your emotions are in control but you're having trouble coming up with the right words, take a strategic delay. Think about what you'd like to say privately, safely, and slowly and then return later.

Finally, if your emotions are in control but you're about to lose your temper, also take a strategic delay. Your grandmother was wrong when she counseled you on the eve of your wedding never to go to bed angry. When you're angry, going to bed may be exactly the thing you need to do to dissipate your adrenaline, regain your brainpower, and prepare to return to the conversation.

CHAPTER SUMMARY

Stay Focused and Flexible

In this chapter we examined how to stay focused and flexible. If fear is the emergent problem, step out of the original infraction, make it safe, and if appropriate, revisit the original problem—returning to the place you left off. If a new issue or problem emerges, choose *what* and *if*. If you decide to deal with the new problem, work through it by following the skills. Then, to ensure that you don't get sidetracked, revisit the original problem—returning to the place you left off.

- When new problems emerge, remain flexible enough to deal with them—without getting sidetracked. Each time you step up to a new problem, it should be by choice not by accident. Choose; don't meander.

- When people feel unsafe, step out of the conversation, create safety, and then return.

- When people don't deliver on a promise because "something came up," deal with this inadequate excuse. Others need to let you know that plans may be changing as soon as they can.

- When a worse problem emerges, step out of the original problem, leave a bookmark so you'll know where to return, and then start over with the new problem. Once you've dealt with the emergent problem, return to the original issue.

- When others become upset, retrace their Path to Action to the original source. Talking about the facts helps dissipate the emotions and takes you to the place where you can resolve the problem.

What Next?

You've dealt with the emergent problem—you've returned to and solved the original problem—and now how do you make sure that you end well? Instead of abruptly halting or fading into oblivion, what can you do to ensure that the effort you've made to hold others accountable will lead to action? That's what we'll explore in the next chapter.

Part Three

Move to Action

What to Do After an Accountability Crucial Conversation

You've talked about broken commitments that are blocking performance—whether the barriers are due to motivation, ability, or both—and come up with a few ideas that will lead to a solution. Now it's time to take these ideas and move to action.

Here's what accountability experts do *after* the conversation to ensure that the problem doesn't keep showing up like a bad penny:

- The best at managing accountability create a complete plan. They build a solid foundation by being specific about what comes next. This includes who does what by when and follow-up (Chapter 7, "Agree on a Plan and Follow Up").

- They piece together all the theories and skills into a complete accountability discussion. They carry a model in their heads and apply it to difficult interpersonal challenges (Chapter 8, "Put It All Together").

- In summary, we'll take a look at how the principles and skills we've learned apply to some very common and complicated issues (Chapter 9, "The 12 'Yeah-Buts'").

7

Agree on a Plan and Follow Up

How to Gain Commitment and Move to Action

By now you've done a lot of work. You noted a violated expectation and decided to talk openly about the gap. You told yourself the whole story and took care to step up to the right issue. You then worked hard to deal with both motivation and ability issues. You even dealt with a new problem, used your bookmark, and then solved the original disappointment. Jointly, you found solutions that seemed promising. Good job!

But don't exhale too quickly. The way you complete the interaction is as important as the way you start it. If you do this well, you build commitment and establish a foundation for accountability. If you don't finish the job—if you swap your backbone for a wishbone—you set yourself up for a whole new set of problems. Let's look at some of these challenges and then explore the skills and tools that accountability experts use to plan and follow up.

PREDICTABLE BAD ENDINGS

Certain bad endings are so common that after you hear no more than a sentence and a half, the whole messy situation comes to mind. For instance, see how long it takes before you can identify where these interactions are headed.

How Good Is Your Crystal Ball?

At the end of last week's meeting, Jane said to Joe, "So you'll get the report done?"

"Absolutely," Joe exclaimed, mentally figuring how to fit another assignment onto a plateful of tasks so overflowing that it was starting to interfere with his bowling.

A week passes, and Jane is at the door: "I needed that report yesterday afternoon. Can I have it now?"

"Now? I had that scheduled for next week," Joe laments.

Jane responds by rolling her eyes: "You must have known I needed it."

Joe hates that eye thing and responds under his breath, "My crystal ball was at the cleaners."

"What was that?" Jane asks, raising her voice.

"Nothing," Joe grunts.

"You said something!" Jane accuses him.

"I said 'My eye is on the ball,' and I mean it!" Joe lies.

What Exactly Is Creativity?

During a formal review discussion, Barb talked to her direct report Johnson about being more creative. Her exact words were, "During the next quarter I want you to use more creativity. You know, come up with more ideas on your own."

In an effort to be more creative, Johnson did indeed come up with more ideas on his own, just as requested. That was the good news. The bad news was that he also implemented many of his ideas without involving Barb or anyone else. He interpreted the request to be more creative as permission to do pretty much whatever he pleased.

When Barb eventually learned that Johnson had changed the company's entire inventory system and hadn't given her so much as a heads-up, she blew a gasket and told him that he had gone well beyond his authority. He responded by arguing that he was just trying to be "more creative" and now she was taking him to task for doing what she had asked him to do all along.

Must We Play Word Games?

Dad is stewing. It's a sultry summer night, and for the last hour and a half he has been staring at the clock. During that time he has tried very hard not to get angry. It's now 1:24 a.m., and his daughter opens the door. Dad shouts, "Shelly, you're really late!"

"No, I'm not, Dad. Last week my friend Sarah didn't come home until nine the next morning; that's *really* late."

"Don't be smart-mouthed with me!" Dad retorts. "You're supposed to be in by midnight, and you've been coming in late all month."

"You're right," Shelly says with a sly smile. "I have been coming in at about 1 a.m. for a month, ever since my birthday. And you haven't said one thing about it at all until now. I thought it was okay."

Dad comes back with his best quip: "Well, ah, ah, hmmm . . ."

DON'T ASSUME

How long did it take before you recognized the problem in these examples? Jane and Joe made a sketchy plan. Without their agreeing on a specific deadline, that plan was doomed from the get-go. They had to play "read my mind" or "take my best guess."

Johnson and Barb faced a different problem. The assignment included who was going to do what by when, but the details about the *what* were not clear. She told him to be creative, but that term is far too subjective. Once again, an accident waiting to happen.

Finally, Dad and daughter represent still another issue. By not confronting his daughter for coming in late (following up on a previous agreement) for several days running, he let Shelly assume that what she was doing must have been okay. Like it or not, Dad had given his tacit approval. At least that was what Shelly thought.

Nailing Jell-O

These problems appear familiar because we create them all the time. We finish a perfectly good accountability discussion and then make sketchy plans that are peppered with vague, unspoken, and unshared assumptions. All bets are off. We can't hold people accountable to do something, sometime, somehow. It's like attempting to nail Jell-O to the wall.

A complete plan, in contrast, assumes nothing. It leaves no detail to chance. It sets clear and measurable expectations (from whence all future accountability hails). It builds commitment and increases the likelihood that we'll achieve the desired results. It also enables both parties better to have the next discussion—for accountability, for problem solving, or for praise.

THE SOLUTION: MAKE A PLAN COMPLETE WITH WWWF

The key to making a complete and clear plan, free from all assumptions (and thus improving a proper accounting), is to make sure to include four key components:

- *Who*
- Does *what*

- By *when*

- *Follow-up*

As we just noted, problems typically arise because assignments have only two or three of these components. Let's look at each of the four and see what the experts (our much valued positive deviants) have taught us from the trenches.

Who

This first issue is the easiest: someone's name has to be attached to each task. But there's the rub. *Someone's* name has to be attached. *Someone* needs to be in charge or accountable. At the end of a meeting, the supervisor says, "Okay, we should get it done by Friday at noon." Come Friday, nothing is done. The boss exclaims, "Where is it?" And the finger-pointing party begins

We is too vague. In business the term *we* is often synonymous with *nobody*. There is no *we* in *accountability*. Parents often make this mistake. Mom says to her kids, "Now before you go play with your friends, let's clean our rooms." Later, to the frustrated mom, the kids whine, "But Mom, you said you'd help."

> For accountability to work, a person needs to know what he or she is expected to do. If the task requires many hands, each person needs to know what his or her part of the assignment is. The "team" can be as ambiguous as "us" or "we." Therefore, when it comes to large jobs, make sure one person is responsible for the whole task and then link specific people to each part.

What

Deciding exactly *what* you're after can be challenging. Johnson ended his performance review with Barb by accepting the responsibility to be more creative during the next quarter. So they followed the rules, right? It was clear who would do what by when. Not exactly. Barb needed to provide a detailed description of the exact behaviors she was looking for: "By being more creative I mean I'd like you to come up with more product ideas on your own. I'd love for you to come to our weekly meeting and present new ideas for improvements. The same is true for solutions. When you see a problem, rather than asking what needs to be done, come up with suggestions and then present them to me."

Ask

When you end an accountability discussion and are deciding exactly what to do, don't take the *what* for granted. Ask if there are any questions about quality or quantity. Ask if everyone has the same characteristics in mind. Ask what might be confusing or unclear that has to be clarified now, in advance.

Contrast

If you suspect that other people are likely to misunderstand you, use Contrasting: "I want you to think of new plans. I don't want you to implement them until we've had a chance to talk, but I do want you to take the initiative to present them." Those of you who have had cataract surgery recently are familiar with the hospital version of this technique. A nurse draws (in magic marker and on your forehead, no less) an arrow over the eyeball that is about to receive the surgery, meaning "this eye, not the other one." When the stakes are high, leave nothing to chance. (How many wrong surgeries were performed until someone came up with this trick?)

By When

Time is a concept of our own construction. It comes with specific names and numbers. It's quantifiable and exact. Thus, when it comes to setting follow-up times or deadlines for change, you'd think there would be no room for confusion. But we find a way. For example, consider the expression "I need it next week." This may be specific. If you are perfectly happy to receive the finished product any time in the next week, you have a clear agreement. Technically, the expression promises nothing before 11:59 p.m. on Saturday. However, if you need it before 5:00 p.m. on Friday, say so. If you need it on Wednesday, clarify. If you need it by noon on Wednesday . . . you get the point.

What makes this issue particularly intriguing is that the more urgent the task and the more critical the timing, the more vague the instruction: "This is hot; I need it ASAP." "Get right on it." "Hey, did you hear me? This baby is top priority. I need it yesterday." These terms of urgency are train wrecks waiting to happen. Think of it this way: "ASAP: the do-it-yourself ulcer kit."

This problem comes up at home too. The following are statements begging for different interpretations: "Don't be late." "I'll get that to you soon." "You need to clean up your mess in the kitchen." We could be wrong about this, but it seems that teenagers have an amazingly well-developed ability to find the cracks in incomplete plans and use them to their advantage. Clarity helps you fill in the cracks.

Follow-Up

Once you've clarified who is supposed to do what and by when, the next step should be obvious: decide when and how you'll follow up on what's supposed to happen. Perhaps both you and the person you are working with have taken an assignment to do something to resolve the problem but things have come up. When it comes to problem solving with your direct reports or children, you don't necessarily want to leave them to their own devices, particularly if the task is difficult and the people who have to deliver on the promise are unfamiliar with the territory. By the same token, you don't want to be checking up on people every few hours. Nobody likes that.

When choosing the frequency and type of follow-up you'll use, consider the following three variables:

- *Risk*. How risky or crucial is the project or needed result?

- *Trust*. How well has this person performed in the past; what is his or her track record?

- *Competence*. How experienced is this person in this area?

If the task the other person has agreed to do is risky, meaning that bad things will happen if it is not done well, and if it is being given to someone who is inexperienced or has a poor track record, the follow-up will be fairly aggressive. It'll come soon and often. If the task is routine and is given to someone who is experienced and productive, the follow-up will be far more casual.

The two most common methods for checking on progress are scheduled and critical-event follow-up times. For routine tasks, schedule a time to see how much progress is being made. Often this is done during a routine meeting at which you'll already be together anyway. With more complicated projects, base the follow-up on milestones or key events: "Get back to me as soon as you complete the initial plan." Or you can combine the two: "If you don't have the plan completed by next Tuesday at noon, let's meet and discuss ways to speed things along."

If you don't have a defined relationship, follow-up can require more creativity. For example, a woman who discussed inappropriate behavior from a male coworker worried that talking about the infraction might not put an end to the behavior, and so she built in a follow-up. She concluded by saying, "Would it be okay if in a month we met in the cafeteria for lunch? I'd suggest our first agenda item be 'Am I acting weird toward you since this discussion?' and 'Has the behavior stopped from my perspective?' What do you say?" This candid, sincere, and respectful request was accepted. And when it was, this skilled woman gained four weeks of clear accountability. The behavior stopped.

If you find yourself in a conversation where you're worried about backsliding, *never* walk away without agreeing on the follow-up time.

Micromanagement or Abandonment

How frequently you follow up with another person depends on that person's record and the nature of the task. How your actions will be viewed by others depends on your attitude and objective. When it comes to following up, ask yourself, "What am I really trying to accomplish?" If you don't trust others, your follow-up methods are likely to be seen as audits ("gotcha!"), and nobody likes an audit.

When people feel as if they're being watched too closely, they tend to transmute into "good soldiers." "Just tell me what to do and I'll do it." They check their brains at the door. They perceive follow-up as criticism. They feel that they are working for a micromanager and are given no chance to show initiative or creativity. In short, the relationship they have with their boss is not based on trust and respect.

Unfortunately, the sense of abandonment people experience at the other end of the follow-up continuum may cause just as many problems. Cutting people loose is certainly more common in today's world of empowerment. Leaders don't want to micromanage. They've felt it, they hate it, and they don't want to deliver it. Micromanaging is bad, and so leaders scarcely follow up at all. Good goal, bad strategy.

Other factors also contribute to an excessively hands-off style. Many leaders (and parents) don't believe they have time to follow up. They give a great deal of freedom to others, even to people who have been fairly unreliable. Nowadays people in authority spend so much time traveling, answering e-mail and text messages, and sitting in meetings that they don't even notice that they don't follow up very often.

Unfortunately, this hands-off style is rarely interpreted positively. People don't say, "I understand. The boss is so busy that he can hardly find time to follow up." More often than not, employees conclude, "The boss doesn't care about me or my project." Busy parents suffer the same fate. Busyness is interpreted as apathy, and this harms both the relationship and the results.

When it comes to how and when you follow up with others, your intentions will have a huge impact.

How about you? If you think you may be at risk of being seen as a person who micromanages or who is too hands-off, check it out. When making an assignment, describe the type of follow-up you think is appropriate. Explain why and be candid about your reasoning. Then sincerely ask if the other person agrees with the method. When you both agree on the frequency and type of follow-up and you both know it, you won't be left wondering if you are being perceived as too hands-off or too hands-on.

Two Forms of Follow-Up: Checkup and Checkback

Who initiates the follow-up discussion? Does the person giving the assignment always take the lead, or are there times when the person taking the assignment follows up? Do a *checkup* when you're giving the assignment and are nervous or have questions. You've looked at the risk, the track record, and the person's experience, and you're feeling anxious or uneasy, even tense. This is the time to use a checkup. You take the lead. Get your calendar out. Say something like the following: "Since this is such an important task, I'm wondering if we could meet next Wednesday at 10 to review how it's going." You write it down. You are in charge of the follow-up.

The fact that you're taking the lead doesn't mean that you are micromanaging. It means that you *own* the follow-up. It can and certainly should mean that you're interested in how the task went, what worked, and what got in the way. If the task is risky enough, the follow-up should be scheduled along the way to make sure that all is going well and that you are available to provide help or coach.

Use a *checkback* when the task is routine and has been assigned to someone who is experienced and reliable. Now that person is in charge. That person checks back. He or she offers suggestions: "How about we follow up at our next scheduled meeting?" or "The deadline is two weeks from today. Could we meet next Thursday 15 minutes before our staff meeting to touch base?"

To achieve the results you want as well as maintain healthy relationships, both checkups and checkbacks can be useful forms of follow-up.

Take Time to Summarize

A planning discussion can be fairly complex and fast-paced, causing us to forget things. Take the time to summarize what's supposed to go down. It could sound something like this:

> *"Let me see if I got this right. Bill, you'll get the nine copies of the report, stapled with a standard company cover sheet, for the meeting Tuesday at 2 p.m. And you'll check back with me before noon that day if you see any problem. Is that right?"*

"Right."

"Can you see anything else that we haven't talked about that might cause a problem?"

When you ask for the other person's input, it can help bring to light issues that might otherwise cause problems. However, the real power of this question goes far beyond clarifying understanding. You're checking for commitment. When the other person eventually says, "I'll do it," that person is much more likely to live up to the agreement. *Never* walk away from a conversation satisfied with a vague nod. If you care about gaining genuine commitment, give the other person the opportunity to say yes to a very specific plan.

AGAIN, FOLLOW UP

First you set a follow-up time:

- Should it be formal? Should it be casual?
- Should it be a checkup or a checkback?
- Should it be based on the calendar or on a critical event?

That's the thinking you do up front. Next comes the actual act of following up. Guess what: The biggest problem with following up is not that we do it too often despite the fact that many of us have felt micromanaged from time to time. The biggest problem is that we don't follow up at all. We set plans, create follow-up dates, and then sort of let them drop. How could that happen?

People Forget

Our first problem is that we tend to forget. Life is so fast-paced, full, and busy, we can't keep all the balls in the air at the same time. How are we ever going to remember to follow up on all the promises that other people make? Or that we make? The answer is that we can't, at least not without help. To keep your promises in front of you, do the following:

- Put follow-up dates and times on your calendar.
- Use sticky notes or computer cues to remind yourself.
- Put follow-up times on your agendas.

Reminding yourself to do what is effective is essential in busy environments and times. Families tend to be particularly bad at this. How many people use computers and other electronic devices when giving assignments to children or loved ones? To most of us that would seem cold and too businesslike: "Dad, I'm your daughter, not an employee." Nevertheless, the times are changing. Find methods, electronic or other.

People Worry

Another reason people frequently fail to follow up on commitments is that they want to be seen as nice. As one interviews people in organizations all over the world, it's interesting how frequently the word *nice* comes up. *Question:* How would you describe your organization's culture? *Response:* Nice. In this case, the word has switched meanings from "pleasant" to "diseaselike."

Nice

adj. A pleasant, nonconfrontational attitude that eventually kills you.

People want to feel at ease, not stressed. Holding others accountable, particularly if you have to be honest, is stressful. So individuals rationalize and choose niceness over following up. It's not a sellout; backing off is the right thing to do.

Of course, you can believe this semitortured logic only if you believe that being honest and holding people to their promises are inherently stressful and bad. Throughout this book we've tried to make the point that people who are good at accountability are both candid and courteous. They are honest but not "brutally honest." You can follow up with people and be a decent human being. In fact, the converse is also true: if you don't follow up, you're being unkind to everyone. Allowing failure eventually destroys results and relationships.

The tools taught in the preceding chapters are designed to help us be candid and nice, get results and be nice, and follow up and be nice. The scripts you can use for following up are both easy and safe. When you follow up, you ask, "How's the Southland project going?" or "We scheduled a follow-up on budget improvements. How's it going?" The purpose of the follow-up is to see what the current status is, how things went, what worked, and what didn't. The intention is to be helpful and supportive.

CHAPTER SUMMARY

Agree on a Plan

We've come to the final element of our skill set. We've done all we can to create safety, and now it's time to Move to Action. First we agree on a plan and follow-up method. Then we actually follow up.

- If we don't end an accountability discussion well, we'll have wasted our time and, worse still, are very likely to disappoint people and create unnecessary anxiety. Assignments will drop through the cracks.

- To end well, become an expert at creating a specific plan that includes who will do what by when. Make sure each person is clearly identified with a responsibility. Make sure the *what* is clearly understood. Call for questions and use Contrasting where necessary.

- Ensure that your plan contains the right and agreed-upon method of following up. The less skilled the person, the spottier his or her history; and the higher the risk, the more frequently you'll follow up. Candidly talk about your follow-up methods.

- Finally, follow up. If things don't go well, step up to the new accountability discussion.

8

*Welcome those big, sticky,
complicated problems. In them are your
most powerful opportunities.*

—RALPH MARSTON

Put It All Together
How to Solve Big, Sticky, Complicated Problems

Now that we've built our entire skill set, let's quickly review each step we covered and then see what the skills look like when applied to a rather big, sticky, complicated problem. This will help us see how a real person during a real conversation might pick and choose from the toolbox of skills we've been building so carefully. Not all the skills will be needed all the time, and so we must have a way of thinking about which skills apply and when and where.

THE BIG IDEA FROM EACH STEP

Choose *What* and *If*

- *What.* Ask yourself what you really want. You can talk about the content, the pattern, or the relationship. To stay focused, ask what you really want.

- *If.* Are you talking yourself out of an accountability discussion? Don't let fear substitute for reason. Think carefully not just about the risks of having the conversation but also about the risks of not having it.

Master My Stories

Instead of assuming the worst and then acting in ways that confirm your story, stop and *tell the rest of the story*. Ask: "Why would a reasonable person not do what he or she promised?" "What role might I have played?" When you see the other person as a human being rather than a villain, you're ready to begin.

Describe the Gap

Make it safe by starting with the facts and describing the gap between what was expected and what was observed. Tentatively share your story only after you've shared your facts. End with a question to help diagnose.

Make It Motivating and Easy

After you've paused to diagnose, listen for motivation and ability. Remember, you rarely need power. In fact, power puts you at risk. Instead, make it motivating and make it easy. To do that, *explore the six sources of influence*. Remember to consider social and structural sources of influence.

Agree on a Plan and Follow Up

Remember who does what by when and then follow up. This idea is simple and serves as its own reminder. Then ask to make sure you're not leaving out any details or missing any possible barriers.

Stay Focused and Flexible

As other issues come up, don't meander; consciously choose whether to change the conversation to the new issue. Weigh the new infraction. If it's more serious or time sensitive, deal with it. If it is not, don't get sidetracked.

Let's see how all these steps apply to an extended example.

IS IT YOU, OR IS IT ME?

For the last six months, Ricky has avoided discussing a potential problem with his wife, Elena, because he's worried that *he* may be at fault. His first wife had cheated on him for a full year before he figured out what was going on. That had rocked him to the core. Not only was he devastated by her infidelity; he reeled at his own inability to spot the early-warning signs of something as serious as adultery.

Ricky was slow to enter another long-term relationship: once bitten, twice shy. That explains why he dated Elena, a friend from church, for four years before convincing himself that his first marriage was a fluke and that Elena was unlike his first wife. Then he took the plunge. After three years of marriage to Elena, Ricky fell into a running debate, constantly bickering— with himself. He began to see signs that maybe something bad, even hideous, was going on behind his back, but he wasn't sure if Elena was acting inappropriately or if he was being unnecessarily suspicious. Thus, Ricky remained silent.

Clearly, Elena had changed. She appeared to be more secretive about her e-mail, quickly exiting from it when he entered their home office. She took more phone calls out of the room than ever before. As Elena successfully explained those behaviors (it was job related and thus uninteresting), a third issue drove Ricky's internal debate to new heights. Elena had begun working a great deal more overtime. This had happened off and on throughout their relationship. But what made extended hours more troubling lately was that her new supervisor was an ex-boyfriend, and some of the late-night work was with him.

Let's walk through this delicate conversation with Ricky. Read the following sections carefully. Two times he'll have to step out of the conversation and restore safety.

CHOOSE *WHAT* AND *IF*

Should He Confront the Gap?

Ricky became crystal clear about the need to have a conversation with Elena when he realized how he and Elena were acting out rather than talking out their problems. His concerns were showing up in a subtle cooling toward Elena. Sensing his withdrawal, she punished him by withdrawing into work. As Ricky considered the clear effect of the absence of conversation on their relationship, he was suddenly certain that he needed to say something. Silence wasn't helping.

What Does He Really Want?

As Ricky thinks about it, he determines that what he really wants is a loving, warm, and enduring relationship with Elena. He doesn't want to accuse her of infidelity and drive a bigger wedge into a struggling relationship. What he should do is discuss what is absolutely true: he is worried about their relationship, both about her loyalty and about his paranoia. This is the topic he chooses to address. Asking what he really wants helps him clarify the issue and avoid spiraling into defensive emotions.

MASTER MY STORIES
Tell the Rest of the Story

Ricky's first challenge is his own mental state. He strongly suspects that Elena is cheating on him. He's almost certain of it. Furthermore, he is certain that if she is being unfaithful, she will lie to cover it up. That's what happened in his first marriage. It's what guilty people do. Because Ricky is so certain that Elena will lie, his natural tendency is to charge in with an accusation, hoping to startle her into revealing something. He'll be able to tell what's really going on by her reaction.

To take control of his emotions, Ricky examines his story. He vigorously attempts to generate alternative explanations for Elena's current behavior. He tells the rest of the story. He does his best to determine why a reasonable, rational, and decent person might do what she's doing. What influences could explain those behaviors beyond the fact that she's a lying cheat? Here are a few of the other factors Ricky considers as he contemplates all six sources of influence:

- Ricky knows that Elena has a strong desire to succeed. She is climbing the ladder at work and is willing to pay the price.

- She may be avoiding talking to him because she worries about having an ugly confrontation.

- He clearly is contributing. He has taken to making sarcastic comments about the time she spends with her boss. He has been much less affectionate lately. Of course she finds less joy in being around him.

- Elena has seemed especially anxious about their expenses. That could be showing up in her acceptance of more overtime.

- Their work schedules are keeping them from spending much time together. That can't be helping.

As Ricky explores alternative explanations, something profound happens to him: he calms down. Of course, he's careful to not let this line of reasoning talk him into blaming himself or withdrawing from the conversation. His goal is simply to balance the "lying, cheating" story with other possibilities. He wants to be able to enter the conversation without adrenaline coursing through his veins, turning him into a slavering moron. The effect of this is significant. The new story creates a sense of curiosity and compassion. He begins to hold his suspicions more tentatively. He still wants to talk but is less inclined to become emotional and leap in with an accusation.

Ricky worries that anything he says about a possible affair is likely to make Elena nervous, and so he decides to start by making it safe. He does that by using his two safety tools: he establishes Mutual Purpose by talking about common ground, and he uses Contrasting to clarify any possible misunderstandings.

MAKE IT SAFE

Establish Mutual Purpose and Use Contrasting

Here's how Ricky begins the conversation:

RICKY: I have some concerns I'd like to discuss. My worry in raising them is that it'll sound like an accusation, and I don't want that. I notice these concerns are affecting our relationship, and I don't want us to feel distant from each other. I think if we could work this out, it would help us get back to how things were until a few months ago. Would that be all right?

ELENA: Works for me. What's been bugging you?

DESCRIBE THE GAP

Once Ricky has done his best to create a safe climate, he tries to describe the gap by starting with the facts and ending with a question. This is how he proceeds:

RICKY: Well, stay with me for a minute here; this'll take a little telling. *(He continues by describing some of the behaviors he saw in his ex-wife and some he is seeing in Elena. As he starts to ask Elena for her point of view, she cuts him off.)*

ELENA: I can't believe what I'm hearing. Are you accusing me of cheating on you? You're so paranoid; this just can't work. *(She starts to leave.)*

MAKE IT SAFE

Obviously, Elena is acting as if she's still feeling unsafe. Ricky will have to continue using his safety skills: reestablishing Mutual Purpose and using Contrasting. Here is how the conversation proceeds.

RICKY: Elena, I know it might sound paranoid. To be truthful, I don't know what's going on. As I've thought about it, I don't think you're cheating, and I'm sorry to make it sound that way. But I'm seeing enough similarities that I can't not worry. I need to talk this through both to find out what's really going on and to find a way to keep my concerns from getting in the way of our relationship.

I don't mean to be offensive, but not talking about it won't work for me. Can we please talk?

ELENA: I'll try. This is pretty hard to listen to.

DESCRIBE THE GAP

Once Ricky has done his best to create a safe climate, he finishes the opening lines by asking a question to help diagnose the root causes of the problem.

RICKY: Can you see how the behaviors I described would lead someone to worry?

ELENA: I suppose. But you don't need to. *(Elena obviously has calmed down and appears ready to discuss the issues honestly.)*

RICKY: Well, I'd like to hear how you view what's been going on.

MAKE IT MOTIVATING AND MAKE IT EASY

Explore the Six Sources of Influence

Ricky tries to understand why Elena is spending less time with him and more time at work with her ex-boyfriend. Here's what he learns:

- Elena has never owed as much money as they currently owe. Her father spent a great deal of time unemployed, and she's anxious about getting behind on their mortgage.

- She didn't want to bring up the money issue with Ricky because she was afraid that she didn't know how to have the conversation without offending him.

- Elena is having a very difficult time working for her boss (her ex-boyfriend) because he seems to be punishing her for breaking up with him by being hypercritical of her work. Plus he's not giving her all the resources she needs.

- Most late nights Elena isn't working with him; she works with her team. She's hoping to feel more secure in her job by overperforming.
- She's been less affectionate with Ricky because she's stressed and tired and because she's noticed his withdrawal.

Ricky and Elena jointly brainstorm solutions that might work. For example, perhaps her financial anxiety would lessen if they dropped their club membership and returned an expensive leased car so that they could start putting away money for a rainy day. She could also look more aggressively at transferring into a less stressful boss-subordinate situation.

As the conversation continues, Elena makes the following sarcastic comment and then goes quiet:

ELENA: I guess *I* can do all the sacrificing again.

STAY FOCUSED AND FLEXIBLE
Don't Meander; Choose

Ricky recognizes the new issue and decides to discuss it. It would appear that Elena feels she's being asked to do more than he is doing, and he wants to explore this point.

RICKY: You're the one who had to make all the accommodations when we first moved here. I didn't realize that was an issue for you. How about if we talk about that and then return to the other topic?

ELENA: I expected you to give up some of your ambitions too. It's been disappointing that you could just let me do all the giving while you do all the taking.

AGREE ON A PLAN AND FOLLOW UP

Decide Who Does What by When and Follow Up

After talking for quite some time, working through some issues, and jointly exploring solutions, they agree on some changes they'll make, clarifying exactly what each person will do and by when. Then Ricky suggests that they talk about it again at the end of the next week and see how things are working both with his worries and with her feelings of not being supported.

CHAPTER SUMMARY

And so there you have it—all the skills applied to a single problem. And here's the good news: it reflects how you and other accountability experts behave on your best days.

A FINAL COMMENT: CAN PEOPLE REALLY DO THIS?

A rocket scientist contemplates talking to her boss about a potential safety problem with a new propellant but chooses not to say a word because she figures that it'll just get her into trouble. For months on end she walks around in a funk, wondering if something horrible will happen. A nurse wonders about making a suggestion to a doctor that could affect a patient's health but holds his tongue rather than incur the physician's wrath. As this unspoken interaction continues, he too lives in a cocoon of worry and doubt. A husband chooses not to question his wife about her suspicious behavior and then lives with the haunting possibility that she may be having an affair.

And so we're back where we started—living the tortured life of the silent majority. We routinely refuse to step up to bad behaviors—despite the fact that they're causing us horrific pain—because we figure that it's better to suffer in the current circumstances than run the risk of saying something dangerous or stupid. It's the same old mental math problem. Here's the formula: if we speak up, we could fail. We also might do nothing to solve the problem. In fact, we could create even worse problems for ourselves. We do the calculations, and the answer that pops into our head is "H-O-L-D Y-O-U-R T-O-N-G-U-E."

But not forever. We suppress our gripes until one day our dark side shows itself. Our ugly stories create a brew that eventually fuels us with enough energy to take scary actions and dumbs us down enough so that we think that what we're about to do is okay, even the right thing to do.

And so we alternate between silence and violence. First we think, "I can't believe I just said that," and so we shut down. Then we think, "I'm not taking this abuse any longer," and so we fire up. This unhealthy cycle might be best described as the social version of quantum mechanics. We jump all the way from silence to violence without ever passing through the intervening space separating the two. We don't pause in the land of crucial accountability, where we converse about violated expectations in a way that eventually solves the problem and improves on the relationship. To us, the lovely place where ideas flow freely and honesty rules doesn't exist. Here's the interesting part: neither silence nor violence serves us, our relationships, or our purposes, and yet we still toggle.

The solution to this reaction to violated promises lies in our ability to step up to high-stakes accountability discussions and handle them well. We see a problem and speak honestly and respectfully. But far more frequently than most of us are willing to admit (like the rocket scientist, the nurse, and the husband), we don't say a word because we don't know how to handle the conversation, or we fear that we don't know how. We're not bad people. We're just frightened. And we're not frightened because we are inherently skittish; we're frightened because we believe failure looms on the horizon. Or so we think.

If only one message emerges from this book, it should be the following: you can step up to a broken promise and handle the conversation well. You already do that on your best days. And when you can take it no longer, you try to do it on your worst days. Now that you have a systematic way to think about accountability discussions and are armed with skills that really work, more days can be your best days.

Equally important, when it comes to holding big, sticky, complicated conversations, you don't have to leap out of a plane without a parachute. Nobody's asking you to take a terrible and irreversible risk. Here's why. The first two skills, "choose *if* and *what"* and "master my stories," take place in the confines (and safety) of your own head. By stepping up to problems that *should* be handled and picking the *right one,* you're ensuring that your effort is worthwhile. By doing your best to keep your emotions under control, you're taking an important step toward acting rationally and reducing resistance and defensiveness. Once again, this is all done *before* you say a single word. No risk there. Also, these actions alone keep you from charging in and ruining the conversation with your first sentence. This alone doubles your chances of success.

You then move from thinking to talking by discreetly and calmly describing the gap. This is the first time you're exposing yourself to any risk whatsoever. But you're doing your best to describe behaviors, not share ugly conclusions. You're a scientist, not a critic or judge. This humanistic approach helps keep the conversation professional and objective.

Now, after sharing one sentence or possibly two, you end with a question, not an accusation. You're not three sentences into the conversation, and you've paused to listen to the other person. This too minimizes the risk. You've observed some things, and you're wondering what's really going on. What's the other person's view?

What if the other person takes offense or maybe even becomes angry and abusive? You can stop and deal with the new problem, or if you're feeling befuddled, you can always take a strategic delay. Back off and take time to rethink your approach. This is a conversation, not a gauntlet. It has exit points.

Let's say the other person responds favorably. He or she doesn't explode or become offended, but merely explains what's happening. He or she is either unable or unmotivated to keep the broken commitment. Or maybe both. That's it.

Consider motivation. This isn't particularly dangerous either. You're not trying to motivate others. You're not trying to figure out how to generate enough power to force others to comply.

Best of all, you're not trying to change underlying, immutable personalities. Your job is simply to make it motivating.

To do this, you jointly explore the forces that cause the task to be motivating or not motivating. This requires you to do nothing more than share natural consequences and listen for the other person to share any additional consequences you may not be aware of. You don't have to pummel people into submission. You may even choose to back off from your original request if it becomes clear that continuing on the original course doesn't make sense. You too can be influenced. When it comes to motivation, you're relying on dialogue, not diatribe.

What if the person isn't able? Once again, your job isn't to force others to do the impossible. By definition, that can't be done. Your job isn't even to force others to do the difficult, not over the long run at least. Your job is to make it easy. How risky is that? Jointly examine forces that are serving as barriers. Jointly come up with resolutions.

It's little wonder that our friend Melissa at the manufacturing plant and the thousands of other positive deviants we studied step up so willingly to accountability discussions. They do this not because they are more courageous than the rest of us but because they are more skilled. They carry different math into the interaction—math that propels them into a virtuous cycle. Their skills lead to success, their success to confidence, and their confidence into trying even more skills, and the cycle continues.

How about you? Are you ready *not* to rumble? Are you ready to hold an accountability discussion that has been keeping you from something you really care about? To give your skill set a final boost, turn to the next chapter, where we look at the ins and outs of several interactions that are both common and challenging. They are the high-stakes conversations that people tend to worry about the most.

9

The 12 "Yeah–Buts"

How to Deal with the Truly Tough

As we've trained this material over the last two decades, we've grown accustomed to people saying, "Yeah, but my situation is really tough. These skills will never work for me." At first we thought those people were being belligerent (particularly when they threw in words like *bonehead* and *hayseed*), but in most cases the concerned participants were only trying to imagine how the skills applied to their world—their toughest world. If the skills could help with their worst-case scenarios, they stood to gain a lot. All they really wanted to do was dive deeper into areas that deserved careful attention. They raised the "yeah-buts" because they were being thoughtful and reflective, in some cases highly reflective.

And so with apologies to the late Stephen R. Covey, a renowned scholar and dear friend, we bring you the seven "yeah-buts" of highly reflective people. And then we add five more, just for good measure.

CONFRONTING AUTHORITY

 "YEAH, BUT... I'M STILL NERVOUS ABOUT *stepping up to my boss and* openly disagreeing or perhaps even confronting her for not following procedure or causing me problems. I could pay dearly and for the rest of my life."

The Danger Point

When it comes to talking about poor performance—and the stakes are high—people tend to err on the side of caution: better to live with your existing circumstances than try to take corrective action, fail, and end up losing *twice*. You're left with the same bad circumstances because nothing has changed, and now the person who holds all the marbles is really upset with you and soon will exact revenge. This isn't merely a problem involving the hierarchy. It could happen with a close confidant or a loved one as well. Loved ones won't fire you from your job, but they can fire you from the relationship, and that can be even more painful.

The Solution

Before we offer some advice, let's be clear about something. Over the years we *have* seen bosses who appeared to be narcissistic or authoritarian to the core. Their very *purpose* appeared to be to stay in absolute control, and anything that threatened that purpose was a threat to them.

In these cases all bets are off. Anything short of groveling will be insufficient. In these cases you have a tough choice to make. You need to choose between coping and cutting out (more on this later).

With that said, we need to be clear about a second point. There are far fewer of these kinds of bosses around than you'd guess from people's complaints. Ninety percent of your boss's defensiveness is largely avoidable. We know because we've seen highly skilled individuals approach people who others thought were clinically controlling *and succeed*.

Here's the bottom line. The people we watched get through to the toughest bosses differed in soul as much as they differed in skill. They were masters at helping their bosses feel safe because they were masters at seeing problems from their bosses' point of view. It was easy for them to create Mutual Purpose because they spent as much time contemplating how the problem behavior they were about to discuss was creating problems for the *boss* as they did fretting about the problems it was creating for *them*. They were incredibly effective at making it motivating for the boss because they had thought deeply about the natural conse-quences of the boss's behavior—on the boss. It's little wonder that the boss welcomed their empowering insight.

Although we don't want to excuse self-centered bosses for their impatience and defensiveness, we do want to suggest that if in reaction to their selfishness we become similarly self-absorbed, we'll never have the insight and compassion we need to succeed. We'll never be able to create enough safety to dis-solve the boss's defenses. Our well-intended conversations will be crushed by the weight of selfishness.

This is *not* a "blame-the-victim" speech. It is about empower-ing the weak. If you want greater influence with a powerful and defensive person, what you typically need is not more power but more empathy. What you need is not a bigger hammer but a big-ger heart. If you can step away from yourself and consider how the problem behavior is affecting *the other person* as well as how it's affecting *you*, you'll have a greater capacity to produce better outcomes for both of you. Besides, people never hammer their bosses without hammering themselves as well.

An Important Aside

Let's get back to choosing between coping and cutting out. When another person is acting in ways that bother you, you have four options. You can carp, converse, cope, or cut out. Carping is the one bad option in this list. You don't really resolve the problem, you hang around and complain, and nothing gets better. Unfortunately, if you complain and moan enough, you harm your own health, not to mention what you're doing to everyone else.

Conversing is your best choice for resolving the issue while building on the relationship. That's what this book has been saying. Coping requires a bit of an explanation. You've done your best to converse respectfully and resolve the problem, but you've been unsuccessful. In fact, you've given up any hope of being successful. Now you can either cope or cut out. Cutting out is obvious. Half of all couples choose this option, and millions of people quit their jobs every year. Coping, in contrast, means that you've decided that the issue isn't big enough to justify ending the relationship. You're not going to divorce your spouse or quit your job, nor are you going to sit around and carp.

To cope properly, you must tell yourself the rest of the story. Most people are reasonable, rational, and decent. You haven't been able to work through your differences because rational people have come to different and *reasonable* conclusions. Your boss isn't an authoritarian moron; she's just trying to make sure that her point of view is taken into consideration. Your husband isn't a selfish idiot; he just forgets to put down the toilet seat in the middle of the night. Forgetting makes him human, not insensitive and uncaring. To cope, you tell the rest of the story and believe it.

Healthy people don't fake coping. They don't hang around and moan, and groan, and complain, and nag, and play "ain't it awful," and wallow in self-pity, and bad-mouth everyone in the known universe, and talk endlessly about being the "big person" who has found a way to show tolerance—and then have the nerve to say that they're coping. No, that is carping, not coping, and carping is the bad option.

BREAKING FROM THE PACK

"YEAH, BUT... THE PEOPLE I WORK with are perfectly comfortable violating standards and turning a blind eye to rules. I usually don't say anything because I don't want to be the odd person out. It's not like you can take on the world all by yourself."

The Danger Point

When you choose to violate a standard practice, depending on the severity of the violation, you're exposing yourself and others to a whole range of risks. For instance, say you're a healthcare specialist watching a doctor go into a sterile area with very sick babies, and he begins to examine them without gloves or a mask. This violation of protocol can lead to infections. Or you're an accountant watching colleagues willfully disobey standard practices to satisfy a customer. This could misinform investors and land you in jail. Or you're an employee watching everyone violate a safety procedure, and nobody says anything because everyone is in a hurry to meet an important deadline.

In each of these cases, you feel as if you're in one of Solomon Asch's conformity studies in which everyone before you says that two obviously different lines are identical and now it's your turn to speak up. Do you do what you think is right and take on your entire work group, or do you go with the flow?

The Solution

The reason you're unwilling to say anything is probably that what you're about to say isn't very pretty. In your view, people are doing what is easy rather than what is right, and in fact they may be doing exactly that. Nevertheless, if you lead with this unsubstantiated accusation, it's not going to go down well:

> *"Hey, are we going to follow the regulations on this, or are we just going to sell out and run the risk of killing some people?"*

As satisfying as this patronizing attack may feel, it's not going to be well received. People may comply, but you've just driven a huge wedge into the relationship. Tell yourself a different story. Maybe others know something you don't know. Maybe they're feeling pressured just as you are. Maybe you just don't know all the facts. Who knows what they're thinking?

One thing is for certain: Seeing yourself as the only one with a conscience or a backbone and then acting on that story is sure to make you come across as self-righteous. It's surely going to provoke other people's resentment and resistance. How could it not? Change your story, and your behavior will change along with it. Ask yourself why reasonable, rational, and decent people are doing what they're doing.

Make It Safe

Open the conversation by acknowledging the competing motivations, and do it in a way that humanizes those who might be leaning in the wrong direction:

> *"I know it's inconvenient to suit up for quick and unobtrusive exams."*

Then use a Contrasting statement to eliminate a possible misunderstanding:

> *"I don't want this to come off as an accusation; it's an honest question. Aren't we supposed to [fill in the blank], or are there circumstances I'm unaware of?"*

These simple sentences take the pressure off you. You don't have to be the police. You don't have to be moral or ethical or stronger willed. You don't even have to be right. You just have to be curious, and that's a good thing.

If people could find a way to use these simple techniques every time they feel peer pressure to do what they know is wrong, they could save millions of dollars, thousands of lives, and countless other forms of suffering.

MARRIED TO A MIME

 MY SPOUSE NEVER wants to talk about anything. I experience a problem with him, and he tells me not to worry or not now or I've got it all wrong, or he just turns back to the TV and says he'll get back to me later. But he never does."

The Danger Point

When relationship researchers asked newlywed couples to talk about a topic that typically leads to an argument, they notice a common pattern among the couples who later ended up divorcing. Not only do those couples use poor techniques when trying to discuss a controversial topic, more often than not one of them tries to work through the issue to its resolution while the other tries to escape.

The fact that one of the pair wants to talk while the other prefers not to is *the* common pattern in strained relationships. Not only can't people talk well, but one cuts off any avenue of resolution, and matters only get worse. This is a big deal.

The Solution

If ever there was a pattern that needs to be confronted, this is it. Any single instance may not seem like that big of a deal, but over time the pattern is killing the relationship. So talk about the pattern.

First, ask if it would be okay to talk about an issue because you think that doing that would strengthen your relationship. You want to be able to talk more openly and freely about problems; your spouse seems to prefer to remain quiet. This is the problem. Fight your natural proclivity to focus on the other person. Instead, acknowledge any complaints the other person may have about what you may be doing to drive him or her to silence. *Hint:* When people move to silence, it's typically because they feel verbally outgunned. If that's the case with you, acknowledge that sometimes you guilt-trip or dominate or hound the other person until he or she succumbs. You want to change this.

When you frame the conversation as an opportunity to solve problems that *the other person* cares about and acknowledge some of the things you've done that might be contributing to the problem, you're creating safety. This, of course, is always the best place to start.

With that done, don't demand that the conversation happen now. Set aside a time to talk. The other person gets to pick when. One of the reasons high-stakes conversations often get sidelined is that the other person isn't emotionally up to it. He or she arrives home from a trip, you've been musing for days, and *bang*, before he or she can catch a breath, a huge issue needs to be resolved. Choose your time carefully. You're going to be talking about a longtime pattern. This topic isn't time sensitive.

When you do converse, share your concerns along with your tentative conclusion that he or she may be purposely avoiding key problem-solving discussions. Don't make this an accusation. Share two or three quick examples and then suggest that this is what is going on. Then prime. Is it because the conversations often don't go well? Is there a way to make sure that they don't end up as arguments? Is there something you can do to make sure that they run more smoothly? Make it safe for the other person to explain why he or she thinks it isn't safe.

Jointly brainstorm things you can do to make sure that you're both comfortable holding relationship conversations. Is your timing wrong? Are you waiting too long and then getting angry? Stick with the brainstorming until you've brought barriers to the surface and found ways to remove most of them. Make this conversational. Lovingly try to resolve the issue. Don't try to "fix" the other person.

HEARSAY

"YEAH, BUT...   *WHAT DO YOU DO when you don't actually see the problem? Coworkers complain endlessly, saying things like 'He's impossible to work with,' 'He can't be trusted,' and 'He never listens to feedback.' How do you handle hearsay?"*

The Danger Point

When people consistently complain to you about a specific employee, you face an interesting challenge. How do you share hearsay? If others are not willing to talk to the person themselves or own up to the negative feedback, you have no right to talk with that person on the basis of secondhand information. That would be both unfair and unhelpful. You're not close enough to the problem to share detailed feedback, and so you end up making general complaints that leave the person upset and confused.

Naturally, if employees complain about something that is dangerous or illegal, you need to consult with human resources immediately.

The Solution

Master your own story. Refuse to accept other people's gossip as fact until you gather firsthand information. When you adopt other people's stories about someone as your own, you surrender control. Observe the bad behavior on your own. Then you can describe it in detail. More important, you can own the story as well. Rather than coming off as a messenger or having to apologize for what others think, you can address the problem head on. People deserve to face their accusers. They also deserve specific, detailed feedback. Anything short of this is unhelpful and unfair. And who knows? As you gather your own data, you may end up with a story different from the one that others attempted to induce you to believe.

The family version of this problem revolves around the ever-present "tattletale." The same principles apply. Unless safety is at risk, gather data on your own. Carry your own message.

POTENTIALLY DEVASTATING

"YEAH, BUT... *WHAT IF THE FEEDBACK you want to give could crush the other person? I've got an employee who thinks she's the world's best writer. She's always begging to compose letters. The truth is that her writing stinks. I don't have the heart to say anything."*

The Danger Point

Most people would rather take a blow to the head than say something that could devastate another person. Telling people that they are incompetent at something they take pride in certainly falls into this category. Bosses often go for years letting people think they're doing a good job when they're not. Then they either make up for the poor job themselves (doing a work-around) or learn to live with substandard work. Both alternatives are unacceptable.

The Solution

If you've allowed a person to operate under the illusion of competency for quite some time, you really aren't in a position to judge whether that person is truly incompetent. You've never held him or her accountable. Begin having accountability discussionss about single areas that could use some improvement. Express your appreciation for the person's willingness. This is something you can praise. Then explain that there is one thing you'd like to see improve. You want to see him or her take the quality in the area you've selected to the next level. Provide clear, direct, and detailed feedback about that area alone. Don't talk about problems per se; talk about setting new standards.

Once the person has improved in that area, pick another problem and work on it. Over time, if the person hasn't been able to improve, and since you've consistently and respectfully held the content conversations and worked to test your assumption about whether he or she is truly incapable of mastering the skill, you will have earned the right to have the larger relationship conversation.

WAY OUT OF LINE AND SCARY

 "YEAH, BUT…" WHAT IF A PERSON *is totally out of line most of the time but threatens to file a grievance if you confront him? And the worst of it is that because of his special circumstances, he'd probably win. Then what?"*

The Danger Point

It's shocking to learn how many companies are stuck with one or more really unproductive employees who hold leaders hostage. Those employees have no interest in doing their jobs, fight legitimate work at every turn, make life miserable for everyone, and have cowed the supervisor. They rattle the saber of litigation, or they imply that they'll take it all the way to the top or that they have dirt on someone. Outsiders routinely ask, "Why is that person still working here?"

The Solution

Resolve to hold the employee accountable. Meet with human resources and jointly develop a plan. Select a behavior that is out of line and indefensible. If necessary, clarify your standards regarding insubordination, resistance, and poor performance. Inform the employee that the action you've selected isn't acceptable and will no longer be tolerated. Simultaneously assure the employee that your goal is for him or her to succeed.

Describe some of the more poignant and relevant natural consequences of the employee's current behavior, such as being stuck in boring assignments and being rebuffed by colleagues. Take care to tell the person what will happen if he or she steps over the line. Once again, make sure that the employee knows that this is not what you *want* to have happen but is a step you will have to take to protect the interests of colleagues and the organization. Document the discussion. Watch the employee closely. Confront the first infraction immediately but respectfully and then start down the path of discipline. Don't be held hostage.

CHANGING YOUR CULTURE

"YEAH, BUT..." WE'RE MAKING A BREAK with the past. It used to be that people looked the other way when you violated policy, but now we're supposed to hold people accountable. How do you change the rules in the middle of the game?"

The Danger Point

Many organizations are just beginning to ask their employees to step up to a new level of initiative, teamwork, customer service, and so on. Unfortunately, despite leaders' efforts to bring about change, slogans, buttons, and banners aren't enough to transform a culture. Calling a group a team doesn't make it a team.

Telling your children they can no longer walk all over you may not reverse the results of a decade of weak parenting.

The Solution

You can't solve longstanding problems if you haven't let others know exactly what you want. With unclear expectations, you don't have the right to hold others accountable to violations they may not even be aware of. Confront the past. Without singling anyone out, outline for people the natural consequences of how things have been. For example, you may describe how saying yes to every urgent demand has caused you to have chronically poor quality and terribly costly operations. As you help people connect consequences with past behavior, you build moral authority for resetting expectations.

Illuminate your general vision of how things are going to be in the future with specific, identifiable, and replicable actions. Clarify dos and don'ts. Study best practices. Contrast what people used to do with what they need to do now. Then teach and focus on those specific actions. If you don't know precisely what you're looking for, you have no right to expect it. Only after you've clarified your new expectation do you have the right to begin having accountability discussions with those who violate the new standards. More than a right, it will then be a responsibility.

BORDERLINE BEHAVIOR

 A WOMAN WHO WORKS for me is always messing up the details. She's not bad enough to be called incompetent, but she's so borderline that you always worry about her work."

The Danger Point

When someone is always doing marginal work, it can test your ability to have a clear and specific accountability discussion:

"Okay, it's not that you didn't respond to the client; it's that you didn't do it in what I would call a prompt fashion and you had a bad attitude when you did respond."

Taking a vague and stilted position like this can be hard to defend and makes you vulnerable to arguments such as "You're never satisfied no matter how hard I try." Now it's your problem, not the other person's.

The Solution

Three factors set those who are adept at dealing with subtle, borderline behavior apart from the rest of the pack: research, homework, and connections.

First, you need to gather data. Have a conversation with the marginal performer about what she likes and doesn't like about her current work situation. What are her frustrations, aspirations, and concerns? Approach your "research" conversation with a genuine desire to discover underlying barriers and then see if you can find ways to resolve them.

Next, scrupulously gather facts—from memory and observation—that will allow you to describe in illuminating detail the difference between mediocrity and excellence. This is crucial. Most people are so vague about that difference that they end up using the feel-good, mean-nothing terms that typically pepper pregame speeches, such as "Your attitude determines your altitude" and "We need you to give 110 percent." This advice may make sense to those giving it but only confuses and insults the people who are supposed to change.

Ask yourself, "What actual behaviors can I describe to make this distinction clear?" Here is an example:

"I notice that after finishing a letter, you skim it once and then hit 'send.' When it's going to an external recipient, I've found that it helps to take three extra steps: read it aloud to see if you've captured what you really want to say, reread it a couple of hours later, and then ask a reliable partner to read it thoroughly."

You will not succeed at helping other people understand the gap between where they are and the vague objective of excellence unless you do the homework required to make your descriptions crystal clear. Carefully gathering useful facts is the homework required for all accountability discussions.

Finally, connect your homework with your research. Explain how your recommendations will not only resolve others' concerns but also help them achieve their aspirations. When you can make this link, your influence will increase enormously. If you can show the other person how the changes you're recommending link to his or her own goals, there's a good chance that the person will be motivated to learn and grow. If you can't do that, don't expect the person to improve.

OUR PLATE IS OVERFLOWING

"YEAH, BUT..." *WHERE I WORK OUR biggest problem can't be discussed in public. We're constantly given more work than we can manage, and then we have to pretend that we're going to do everything. If you express your concern aloud, you're treated like you're not a team player."*

The Danger Point

Here's a trick for getting people to do things you could never ask them to do without getting in trouble. The various branches of the military have been using this technique for years: they encourage recruits who are a few weeks ahead of the brand-new initiates to abuse their peers in ways that people in official positions of authority could never get away with. People will do things to their coworkers that would land their bosses in the slammer if they did the same things.

This is exactly what organizations do when nobody in authority ever says a word, writes a policy, or publishes a document that calls for an unhealthy workload. Who could do such a thing? Instead, bosses make unrealistic demands and then count on the fact that everybody will sit there and take it. Although it's true that leaders may use their influence to push people to work insane hours or take on insane workloads, if employees put up with the abuse or watch others put up with it, everyone becomes a party to the problem. It's a conspiracy of silence.

If new employees speak their minds about issues of work-life balance, they're acutely aware of the fact that if they say something in public, they aren't merely questioning the boss; they're going toe-to-toe with the entire "culture." And if they take on the culture, they won't be seen as "team players."

The Solution

This is a conversation that has to start with Mutual Purpose. Go straight for the issue of being a team player:

> *"I'd like to talk about a subject that most people don't seem comfortable discussing in public. My goal is to make sure that we're all able to contribute to the company and meet our objectives. I want to be a team player, and I want to understand what that takes."*

Next, blend facts and your tentative conclusions:

> *"There are times when I feel like we're taking on assignments with deadlines we know we can't keep. I know I do. We look around the room, and nobody is saying anything, and*

*so we all smile politely and agree. I get the sense that we're
hoping that others won't be able to meet their obligations, and
then, if they speak up first, we won't get in trouble for missing
our deadlines. It's like playing chicken. Who will be the first to
turn away from the head-on collision of a massive assignment
soon to meet an impossible deadline? Could we talk about
this subject, or am I the only one who sees it this way?"*

At this point you'll have to explore all the underlying sources
that are leading to a culture of impossibility. Don't point fingers;
look for causes. Remember, the world around you has been perfectly organized to create a culture in which smart people are
doing stupid things. What are you doing to each other? How
many of the issues are structural? What's going on in the environment that's forcing people into such unfavorable circumstances?

This is a huge issue. It's causing more stress with more people
than most of us might imagine. As international competition
increases and resources continue to be cut, hours increase. The
workload goes from doable, to nearly impossible, to a joke.
We're now overworked, stressed, and dishonest.

One Final Note

This is probably a conversation you want to have with several
people in private before bringing it up in public. Unlike just
about everything we've talked about until now, this is not a
problem that is solved one-to-one because it's part of the whole
culture. But it is a problem that is best prepared one-to-one.
Meet with several colleagues. See if others share your concerns.
If they do, ask them to share their honest opinions when you do
bring up the issue. Then go public.

I DON'T WANT TO BE A NAG

*I KEEP BRINGING UP THE SAME problems over and
over, and my spouse and children continue in their old
ways. It makes me feel like a nag, and I don't want
to be a nag."*

The Danger Point

Nagging is the home version of Groundhog Day. People repeatedly break a commitment. We talk about the original infraction, but we don't address the bigger issue: they're continually making commitments and not keeping them.

The Solution

The second time a person fails to pick up her clothes off the bedroom floor or doesn't put his dishes in the dishwasher or continues to squeeze the toothpaste in the middle of the tube, you have a new problem: That person has failed to live up to a promise. You are at a crossroads. You can converse about the pattern. You can nag. You can cope.

Toothpaste tubes and dishes in the sink are the stuff nagging is made of: minor infractions, often repeated and often reprimanded. Nobody ever says, "My wife is such a nag. Every time I have an affair with a woman half my age, she makes a big deal about it." Big issues, often repeated, are ongoing disasters. Little issues, often repeated—that's nagging. Choose your battles.

If the original issue continues to bother you, talk about the pattern, but only if the original issue is worth it. Sometimes the infraction is just not worth the aggravation. This is a toothpaste tube we're talking about. Maybe you should expand your zone of acceptance. If you choose to cope, explain to the other person that you've decided that it's not worth arguing about the issue. You would prefer that he or she not squeeze the toothpaste tube in the middle, but you're not going to bring it up again. Then let it go.

OUR RELATIONSHIP IS BASED SOLELY ON PROBLEMS

 "YEAH, BUT..."

I WORK WITH A PERSON who is constantly making mistakes. Every conversation we have is about a problem. I get the feeling that he no longer listens to

me. I walk in the room and the guy bristles. How do I problem-solve with a person with whom I have such a one-sided relationship?"

The Danger Point

It's hard to make it safe to talk about performance gaps when you have no relationship with the other person save for the occasional accountability discussion. Like it or not, every relationship has a tipping point. When the majority of your conversations turn into holding an accounting, the other person starts to wait for the other shoe to drop, no matter the topic, no matter your intent. You cease to be a force other than a nag.

The Solution

Get to know people under less strained circumstances; it matters a great deal. In fact, three separate studies conducted by the authors revealed that the single best predictor of satisfaction with supervision is frequency of interaction. And if your interactions are infrequent *and* only about problems, you're really doomed. Every accountability discussion starts off on the wrong foot. Others only hear your position; they never see you as a person.

So go out of your way to create a wider range of interactions. And when you do interact, feel free to let down your business persona and connect at a personal level. The very first leadership study the authors conducted revealed something rather astonishing. When those who were viewed by senior managers as top performers showed outsiders around their work area, they introduced their employees. They bragged about them. They shared interesting tidbits about their children. "Kelvin's son is at the Naval Academy." They had obviously talked about a whole host of topics and developed a personal relationship. Bottom performers, in contrast, showed outsiders the equipment and products. They walked right by their people as if they weren't even there.

So develop more full relationships. Take people to lunch. Don't have an agenda—just talk. Walk around and casually chat about topics that interest the other person. And when you see "things gone right," recognize people for doing a good job. Become a whole person, and not just a purveyor of problems. Create a healthier context for solving problems when they do come up.

As far as your family is concerned, if you don't take a break from your busy schedule and take your teenagers to lunch, with no purpose other than hanging out together, you'll eventually pass the family tipping point. No matter how wrong they may be or how often they may cause problems—no matter how called-for the conversation—at some point you'll be seen as little more than an uncaring nag. Your motive will always be suspect. Your ability to have a broader influence by holding meaningful conversations becomes severely limited. So don't pass the tipping point. The more often others let you down, the harder you'll have to work to create a well-balanced relationship.

I DON'T THINK WE CAN CHANGE

"YEAH, BUT... *THESE ARE LIFELONG PATTERNS we're talking about. I'm not sure that I or any of the people around me can actually change. Reading is a lot easier than actually acting differently."*

The Danger Point

It's easy to get discouraged when staring into the face of habit. When it comes to human interaction, much of what we do, we do almost without thinking. We follow lifelong scripts: well worn, familiar, and nearly automatic. We lay into our kids with the same ease and lack of thought typical of ordering fast food. We know what we're going to say, we know what others are going to say, and we don't even have to think about it. We could play either part.

How do you break away from lifelong habits?

It's also easy to get discouraged when we know that we tried to make improvements in the past and failed. Ninety percent of those of us who have attempted to lose a few pounds have dropped and then regained the same weight so many times that we no longer believe our own stories: "This time I'm going to keep it off for sure. This time it's different." Or maybe it's been an exercise program that has yielded a different mechanical contraption every year until the garage is bursting with nearly new aerobic ab machines, and yet we still break into a sweat trying to open a jar of pickles. Or perhaps we made a commitment to eating healthier foods but sort of lost steam when we found ourselves stopping at a Fat Burger for a pick-me-up on the way to the health food store.

Accustomed to talking ourselves into short-term action that can't be sustained, we become cynical self-doubters who are reluctant to start down one more trail we'll never follow to the end.

So how do we stick to a plan?

The Solution

The good news is that nothing in this book is new or the least bit alien. The skills we teach weren't discovered on the planet Krilnack. On your best day you do much of what every interpersonally smart person does. You step up to accountability discussions, work hard to ensure that you don't fly off the handle or otherwise act stupid, and do a pretty good job. On your best day you are the kind of person the authors were studying when they isolated the best practices for dealing with failed promises.

You don't have to change everything—just a few things—and maybe be a bit more consistent. Better still, you don't have to change your underlying, immutable, "I-can't-help-it-if-I-was-born-this-way" personality. To improve your results, you need to reshape a few of your thoughts and alter a few of your actions. That's it. There is no need for a full-fledged genetic intervention, and frontal lobotomies are out of the question (save for recreational purposes).

To make this "tweaking of thoughts and words" easier, we have a few suggestions. First, studying this book is best done in pairs. Find one or more other people and share ideas. Develop goals, practice together, and support each other as you step up to new and untested accountability discussions.

Whether you're working in pairs or alone, pick one skill and work on it. Then do the same thing with another skill. Devote one hour a week for 10 weeks. That's all it takes to bring about important changes. Set aside a time at home and at work when you will talk about infractions that normally you would leave untouched. Finally, check out the support materials available at http://www.vitalsmarts.com/bookresources. Download the free material. Watch the videos. Sign up for ongoing assistance and reminders. Pick one skill and work on it for a week.

JOIN THE *CRUCIAL SKILLS NEWSLETTER* COMMUNITY

Was your most pressing question left unanswered? Subscribe to our free weekly e-newsletter and ask your own tough "yeah-but" questions. The authors answer reader's questions with powerful insights into tough, real-world accountability discussions. Sign up today at http://www.vitalsmarts.com/bookresources.

Appendix A

Where Do You Stand?

A Self-Assessment for Measuring Your Accountability Crucial Conversation Skills

WHERE DO YOU STAND?

To measure your skill level and see how this book can best serve your needs, candidly review the following statements. Check "yes" if they apply to you. Check "no" if they do not.

A self-scoring version of the following assessment is available at http://www.vitalsmarts.com/bookresources. There you'll also find tools to assess how well your family, team, and organization handle accountability discussions.

Choose *What* and *If*

Yes No

☐ ☐ 1. To avoid getting into an argument, I tend to put off certain discussions longer than I should.

☐ ☐ 2. Sometimes when people disappoint or bother me, I confront them—only to realize that I talked about the easy problem, but not the real root problem.

Yes No

☐ ☐ 3. Parts of my life would improve if I could just figure out how to talk about certain hot topics without taking too much risk.

☐ ☐ 4. Occasionally I talk myself out of holding a certain discussion by convincing myself it's better to cope than it is to risk an ugly confrontation.

☐ ☐ 5. With some of the problems I care about the most, I find myself bringing up the same issue over and over again.

Master My Stories

Yes No

☐ ☐ 6. When others do things that are mean or selfish and I'm less than kind in return, I tell myself that they deserved it.

☐ ☐ 7. When others don't deliver on a promise, there are times when I judge their reasons for doing so more quickly than I should.

☐ ☐ 8. Sometimes I assume that others cause me problems on purpose, and then I act as if this assumption is actually true when it may be false.

☐ ☐ 9. Occasionally I wonder if I'm too quick to anger.

☐ ☐ 10. There are times when I've totally blamed others for a problem only to learn that I was partially responsible.

Describe the Gap

Yes No

☐ ☐ 11. Sometimes I bring up problems in a way that makes others defensive.

☐ ☐ 12. Occasionally I talk to someone about his or her bad behavior within earshot of others.

Yes No

☐ ☐ 13. There are times when I can't figure out how to give others completely honest feedback in a way that won't offend them.

☐ ☐ 14. Sometimes when I bring up a problem, I do too much talking and not enough listening.

☐ ☐ 15. When I bring up problems with others, there are times when I make it hard for them to share their views.

Make It Motivating

Yes No

☐ ☐ 16. I can't motivate some of the people to change because I don't have enough power to do so.

☐ ☐ 17. In order to get people to want to do certain things, sometimes I rely on guilt or even threats.

☐ ☐ 18. There are times when I can't figure out why people aren't interested in doing what they should be doing.

☐ ☐ 19. Sometimes it's hard to get others to understand that the behavior I want from them is really in their best interest.

☐ ☐ 20. There are people I routinely deal with who, to be honest, just can't be motivated.

Make It Easy

Yes No

☐ ☐ 21. When people find a job to be unattractive or noxious, I occasionally turn up the heat so they'll do it no matter what.

☐ ☐ 22. When someone can't do something, I tend to jump in with my advice, when all they really want is a chance to talk about their ideas.

Yes No

☐ ☐ 23. Sometimes I think that individuals who bend over backward to make jobs easy are pampering people who just need to do their job and be held accountable.

☐ ☐ 24. Occasionally after finishing a problem-solving discussion, I forget to check to see if the other person is committed to doing what's necessary.

☐ ☐ 25. There are times when I've asked others for their ideas but didn't really need them because I already had a plan of my own.

Stay Focused and Flexible

Yes No

☐ ☐ 26. When talking to others about problems, sometimes I get sidetracked and miss the original problem.

☐ ☐ 27. When people bring up whole new problems during an accountability discussion, I don't know what to do with the new issue.

☐ ☐ 28. When people get angry in the middle of a discussion, I don't always know how to respond.

☐ ☐ 29. I'm pretty good at staying focused on an issue, but occasionally I may miss talking about what the other person really wants to discuss.

☐ ☐ 30. When people miss a commitment and should have updated me but didn't, I generally let them off the hook—even though they didn't have the courtesy to involve me.

Agree on a Plan and Follow Up

Yes No

☐ ☐ 31. Sometimes I work through a problem but forget to clarify who is supposed to do what by when.

Yes No

☐ ☐ 32. There are times when I'm disappointed with what others have done because they have failed to understand exactly what I wanted them to do.

☐ ☐ 33. Sometimes I neglect to give others a specific deadline, only to be surprised when they don't deliver by the time I expected them to.

☐ ☐ 34. I'm pretty sure that either my kids, my spouse, or some of the people I work with think I micromanage them.

☐ ☐ 35. Sometimes I give people assignments but don't have adequate time to follow up.

Scoring

Add up the number of boxes you checked "yes." Each represents an area where you could use some assistance. Here's what your total score means:

26–35: Don't put this book down!

16–25: You could use some help, but at least you're honest.

6–15: You're capable and likely are succeeding.

1–5: You could teach us all a thing or two.

Chapter-by-Chapter Results

This survey is divided into the seven chapters that cover crucial accountability skills (five questions each). Look at your results chapter by chapter. You may want to focus your attention on the chapters where you checked the most "yes" boxes. These chapters offer the solutions to your most common challenges.

Appendix B
Six-Source
Diagnostic Questions
The Six-Source Model

The six-source model helps us expand our view of why people do what they do. By looking at all six sources, we can expand our traditional thoughts about why people do the things they do ("They enjoy causing problems!") to include each person's ability along with the social and environmental factors behind all behavior.

To help dive deeper into each of the six sources, we are providing the following list of exploratory questions. These diagnostic questions in turn help each of us answer the questions "Why the gap?" "Why did the other person let me down?"

SOURCE 1. SELF, MOTIVATE (PAIN AND PLEASURE)

Others take pleasure from the current behavior or find the desired behavior to be painful.

Diagnostic Questions

- Do they enjoy doing what has been asked? Does performing the task in and of itself bring them satisfaction?
- Do they take pride in their work and their work habits?
- Is the required task boring, noxious, repetitive, physically or mentally exhausting, or painful?
- Are they doing the wrong thing because they enjoy it more?

SOURCE 2. SELF, ENABLE (STRENGTHS AND WEAKNESSES)

They don't have the knowledge or ability to perform the required task. They feel more capable performing a different task.

Diagnostic Questions

- Do they have accurate and complete information?
- Are they able to perform the mental tasks?
- Are they able to perform the physical tasks?
- Are they doing the wrong thing because they don't feel more capable in this than in doing the right thing?

SOURCE 3. OTHERS, MOTIVATE (PRAISE AND PRESSURE)

Other people (friends, family, coworkers, and bosses) punish the right behavior while praising the wrong behavior.

Diagnostic Questions

- Does doing the right thing draw no attention or even disdain from the people they care about?
- Are their coworkers pressuring, embarrassing, or provoking them into the wrong behavior?
- Is their boss giving other tasks a higher priority or not supporting the right behavior?
- Does completing the job put them at odds with their family and friends?
- Am I doing something that discourages them?
- Am I failing to do something that would encourage them?

SOURCE 4. OTHERS, ENABLE (HELPS AND HINDRANCES)

Other people make it hard or impossible to do the right behavior while making it easy to do the wrong behavior.

Diagnostic Questions

- Are others withholding information?
- Do others provide them with the resources they need?
- Are others providing help when needed?
- Have others provided adequate permission or authority?
- Am I doing something that inhibits them from succeeding?
- What help or resources should I be giving that would make it easier for them?

SOURCE 5. THINGS, MOTIVATE (CARROTS AND STICKS)

The formal reward structure encourages the wrong behavior while discouraging the right behavior.

Diagnostic Questions

- Will doing the right thing cost them money?

- Does doing the right thing put their career or job at risk?

- Does doing the right thing put better jobs, assignments, or working conditions at risk?

- Does doing the wrong thing bring them more money, enhance their career, or give them better assignments or working conditions?

SOURCE 6. THINGS, ENABLE (BRIDGES AND BARRIERS)

The environment, structure, policies, procedures, rules, and all other "things" make it hard or impossible to do the right behavior while making it easy to do the wrong behavior.

Diagnostic Questions

- Is the required task part of their current job description or role?

- Are there policies, rules, or procedures that make the desired behavior difficult or impossible?

- Are their bureaucratic steps or barriers that hinder them?

- Do they have the equipment or tools they need?

- Is the physical environment a help or a hindrance?

- Do they have access to the information they need—are they getting adequate performance feedback?

- Are their goals and priorities clear?

Appendix C
When Things Go Right

Crucial Accountability was written to address the question of how we confront and address a gap in our expectations. Let's take a look at the other potential outcome we haven't explored yet: The other person has performed up to expectations or even better. This is your chance to express sincere praise.

PRAISE

Praise plays an important role in problem solving. Those who are best at holding accountability discussions make good use of praise between conversations. When people see them coming, they already feel respected and valued. They assume that the problem solver has their best interests in mind because he or she consistently recognizes when things are going well and talks about those accomplishments openly and frequently. When given sincerely and often, praise provides a reserve of respect one can draw from when it's time to talk about a failed promise.

Praise is also a subject that receives attention about twice a year when human resources folks conduct satisfaction surveys. According to the authors' research, the number one employee complaint year in and year out always comes down to the same issue: not being recognized for a job well done. It seems that most of us are missing opportunities to create a climate of mutual respect. To help reverse this trend, let's look at some thoughts about praise that are a bit counterintuitive.

Counterintuitive Suggestions

Praise More Than You Think You Should and Then Double It

When it comes to giving out praise, we're all suspicious. When someone suggests that perhaps we should be more generous in giving praise to others—say, employees, loved ones, and children—we worry about going overboard. We don't want to cheapen our praise by doling it out so liberally that it no longer means anything. So we hold our praise for special occasions such as Olympic medal ceremonies, retirement parties, and funerals. After all, there can be too much of a good thing.

Perhaps the biggest reason we don't mete out praise very often is that we miss the chances to do so. We don't see the positive. For example, when your kids *aren't* fighting, you don't notice it. When your direct reports are plugging along day in and day out and aren't causing problems, who could notice that? In fact, Sherlock Holmes once solved a crime because he alone observed that a dog wasn't barking. You have to be a fictional genius to notice the absence of noise. The same thing is true with problems. And if you don't notice the lack of problems ("things gone right"), you certainly won't praise people.

The fact that the praise statistics never get better no matter how much we study them, talk about them, and lament their embarrassing consistency is a function of the fact that our society suffers from obscured vision—we can only see the bad. In the leadership literature this is called management by exception: pay attention to and work on things gone wrong. Within a family it's called survival: put out the fire before it consumes the house. Every year people complain that they aren't recognized for their good performance because every year their bosses are so blinded by problems that they don't notice things that have gone right.

Of course, we do notice record-breaking accomplishments. Hit new numbers or finish a huge task, and the world takes notice. But honoring the humongous or the exceptional is expected. It doesn't feel like genuine praise; it feels like getting your due. Celebrating mammoth accomplishments will never satisfy an individual's desire for more praise.

To put this problem in perspective, Mark Twain once suggested that he could live for two months on a good compliment, and he was an American hero during his lifetime. How much more do everyday heroes such as file clerks, code writers, and prison guards long for a simple word of thanks? And what will it take to be able to first see and then celebrate achievements other than record-breaking performances?

The psychological explanation for our inability to see things gone right is incorporated in figure-ground theory. The human perceptual system simplifies any visual array into a *figure* that we look at and a *ground* that is everything else that makes up the background. In corporate and family life, problems are the figure and everything else is the ground.

M. C. Escher made a better living than most of his contemporaries by painting works that confused figure and ground. First you see the black birds, and then you squint your eyes just so and see the white birds. We would all make life better if we ensured that certain aspects of human behavior were more noticeable and thus noticed, turning routine success into something that first catches our eye and then gets attention.

As in squinting at an Escher painting, we must find ways to reverse what has historically been background and turn it into the foreground, the focus of our attention and the object of our good words. What would it be like if our employees, loved ones, and children felt that we always noticed their hard efforts and good works? What would it be like if our own companies and families were known as places where good deeds were rewarded instead of punished?

To achieve this monumental feat, to turn around more than a half century of low praise scores, requires but three things: commitment, a change in standards, and simple cues.

An illustration might help. Let's take our lead from Donald Petersen, former chairman of Ford Motor Company. Every day he sat down at a massive desk—in an office large enough to shoot hoops in—and handwrote short, sincere, positive messages to people he worked with. He argued, "The most important ten minutes of your day are those you spend doing something to boost the people you work with."[1]

Here was the chairman of one of the largest companies in the world, a man who easily could have spent all his time doing long-term planning and high-level thinking, and he believed that his most important job was to offer sincere appreciation to those around him. That's the change in belief we're suggesting. Until we buy into the notion that expressing honest appreciation as a leader, friend, and parent is one of our most important jobs, we're not likely to do much to overcome the mental mechanisms and years of habit that keep us focused on problems.

The second feature of what Mr. Petersen did is also worth noting. He sent simple handwritten notes. If you talk to anyone who received one, you're likely to learn that the notes often commented on modest accomplishments. He didn't thank people only for home runs; he thanked them for cheering from the bench or quietly offering support. Our current standards for recognition contain two enormous barriers. First, the feat must be monumental. Second, the reward must match; it should be expensive and time-consuming. Break the habit. Look for and then praise small things. Most of us are already celebrating the big things.

Husbands often have a hard time getting this point. When all a wife really wants is a kind word, a gentle touch, or a sincere smile, the husband misses these opportunities for months on end and then one day ponies up with a new car. Or worse, he gives her something he thinks is terrific but she doesn't. The prize for this version of insensitivity goes to a fellow who gave his wife a manhole cover for Valentine's Day because it had her initials pressed into it (CON for "City of Newark"). "Wow, my very own manhole cover/jewelry! Does it come with a chain?"

The third element is a bit harder to notice. The chairman of Ford sat down *every day* and wrote notes. By doing it every day, he didn't have to be reminded. Even if we sincerely want to reward accomplishments and are willing to look for the little things, we often forget. Problems are the field, and solutions are the ground. To reverse this habit, schedule time to do nothing but focus on things gone right. Set aside a time every day to walk around and look for elements that you can praise. Then do it. Sit down at your computer, bring up the e-mail address of a friend or colleague, and write a thoughtful note. Keep it short and sincere. With time and practice, you'll start noticing things gone right more naturally.

If we're paying attention to small accomplishments and then offering up thanks or perhaps a note or maybe a tiny memento, aren't we being too low-key and cheap? Consider the following story: Every year one of the authors receives a birthday card with a handwritten message from an old friend. He hasn't seen this friend in over a decade, and yet every year a card shows up in his mailbox. It's nice. It's the only card other than ones from family members he ever receives, and it always contains a thoughtful personalized note. Sometimes the author picks up the phone and calls his old friend. Sometimes he fires off a thank-you e-mail. But mostly he just reads the card, thinks of the pleasant friendship, and smiles the smile of a person being appreciated. Small, heartfelt moments of appreciation never wear thin.

Surely the person who sends the card has a reminder on his calendar. That's the cue. Surely he cares about being pleasant and thoughtful. That's the commitment. And surely he realizes that just having a birthday is cause enough for a thoughtful word. That's the change in standards.

Praise Individuals in Private and Groups in Public

This notion also runs counter to what typically happens in organizations. The whole idea behind every award ceremony ever devised is to allow people to bask in the admiration of their friends and peers. That is a good thing. Research reveals, however, that when this is handled poorly, many people feel resentment toward the people who are being honored. "Why wasn't I picked?" is a common question. When you can, celebrate team successes as a team and private successes in private.

Focus on the Process, Not the Results

This runs counter to what typically happens. Teams and individuals alike are often rewarded for breaking records. The danger is that in doing this people also break all kinds of rules, regulations, and policies just to hit the higher numbers. Sometimes they merely cook the books. This is not to suggest that numbers don't matter but to highlight the importance of rewarding individuals who stick to effective processes.

For example, a group of waitresses at a Matsushita plant in Tokyo received the Presidential Gold Medal for saving money on the tea they served in the company cafeteria.[2] The waitresses noted who typically sat where and how much tea they consumed and then poured the appropriate amount at each table. They didn't save the most money—not by a long shot—but earned the award because they followed the process better than others did.

Add Spontaneity to Structure

We've nibbled at this issue; now let's take a big bite out of it. Most of the recognition handed out in companies is structured. We hold monthly awards ceremonies; we have annual banquets.

When these events become the only venue for honoring our friends and colleagues, people become cynical. Recognition feels obligatory and insincere. Praise feels mechanical and cold. Simple, sincere, and individualized handwritten notes are replaced by fancy etched plaques that are written once, carved by machines, and applied equally to everyone.

Supplement your formal celebrations with 10 times as many informal ones. Write personal notes, stop people in the hall, drop off a cookie or flower, and make "thank you" your mantra. Watch for things gone right and then spontaneously and sincerely offer up your thanks and praise. Tell people what they did and why it's worth noting and then end with a simple "Thank you."

Make recognition such an informal, spontaneous, important, and common part of your corporate and family culture that formal celebrations will feel heartfelt rather than mechanical and obligatory. Make praise such a common part of your personal style that when you do enter into an accountability discussion, you'll have built a safe, trusting, and respectful relationship.

Appendix D

Discussion Questions for Reading Groups

Move from "thinking about it" to "got it" with a regular discussion of *Crucial Accountability*. Organize a small group of family members, friends, coworkers, or colleagues and hold a weekly discussion. Here's a short list of questions sure to kick-start any group discussion.

For a downloadable version of the discussion questions found in this book, visit http://www.vitalsmarts.com/bookresources.

1. Behind the serious and long-lasting problems that families, teams, or organizations typically face are accountability discussions that people either aren't holding or aren't holding well. Explain.

2. What are the accountability discussions you typically avoid? What performance gaps have you had the courage to step up to but have handled poorly?

3. When deciding if they should hold an accountability discussion, what tricks do people typically employ in order to talk themselves out of speaking up? What tricks do you use most often? What will it take for you to break the silence-to-violence habit?

4. When deciding what to confront, what mistakes do people typically make? How does the term "Groundhog Day" apply to accountability discussions?

5. Someone has let you down. You figure he or she did it on purpose, and so you're about to give the person a piece of your mind. Why is it that you are now you at risk of making the situation worse?

6. Why are the first few seconds of an accountability discussion so important? What mistakes do people typically make when first describing a performance gap?

7. What motivates people and why? When it comes to motivating others, what mistakes are people in positions of power likely to make?

8. When people aren't able to deliver on a promise, what mistakes might a new leader or parent make? When others are blocked from performing, why ask them for their ideas on how to solve the problem? Why should you "make it easy" for others?

9. You're talking about a problem, and a new one comes up—what should you do? If you decide to deal with the new problem, when are you merely being distracted? When are you being sensible and flexible?

10. What principle from this book did you find most important? Which one was the most surprising?

11. What skill did you find to be the most difficult to put into practice? Why was that? What will it take to get better at that skill?

12. How can your discussion group help each member become better at holding accountability discussions?

13. How can you help one another prepare or practice for a particularly difficult conversation?

14. What methods can you use to remind yourselves to be on your best behavior—particularly when you're becoming upset and are about to move into "lecture mode"?

Notes

Introduction

1. VitalSmarts study: *When Bad Relatives Happen to Good People* (July 2009).

2. VitalSmarts study: *How to Talk Politics with Friends—and Still Have Some Left* (September 2012).

3. VitalSmarts study: *Corporate Untouchables* (September 2006).

4. VitalSmarts study: *Pssst! Your Corporate Initiative Is Dead and You're the Only One Who Doesn't Know* (February 2007).

5. Deborah Tannen, "How to Give Orders Like a Man," *New York Times Magazine* (August 28, 1994): 201–204.

6. Richard P. Feynman, *What Do You Care What Other People Think?* (New York: Bantam Books, 1988), 214–215.

Chapter 1

1. Paul Ekman, *Emotions Revealed: Recognizing Faces and Feelings to Improve Communication and Emotional Life* (New York: Henry Holt and Company, 2003).

2. Solomon E. Asch, "Effects of Group Pressure upon the Modification and Distortion of Judgments," in Harold S. Guetzkow, ed., *Groups, Leadership, and Men* (Pittsburgh, PA: Carnegie Press, 1951), 177–190.

3. Stanley Milgram, *Obedience to Authority: An Experimental View* (New York: Harper & Row, 1974).

Chapter 4

1. Kurt Lewin, Ron Lippett, and Robert White, "Patterns of Aggressive Behaviour in Experimentally Created 'Social Climates,'" *Journal of Social Psychology* 10 (1939), 271–299.

2. Yuichi Shoda, W. Mischel, and P. K. Peake, "Predicting Adolescent Cognitive and Social Competence from Preschool Delay of Gratification: Identifying Diagnostic Conditions," *Developmental Psychology* 26 (1990), 978–986.

Appendix C

1. Fred Bauer, "The Power of a Note," in *Heart at Work: Stories and Strategies for Building Self-Esteem and Reawakening the Soul at Work*, compiled by Jack Canfield and Jacqueline Miller (New York: McGraw-Hill, 1998), 190–194.

2. Masaaki Imai, *Kaizen: The Key to Japan's Competitive Success* (New York: McGraw-Hill, 1986), 19–20, 107.

Index

A

Abandonment, 203–204
Ability:
    confusing motivation and, 139–143
    link between motivation and, 138–139
    motivation vs., 153
    power of single barrier to, 153–154
Ability barriers, 224
    brainstorming to eliminate, 154–156
    joint exploration of, 145
    motivation barriers and, 153, 159–160
    positive deviants' response to, 11
    power of single barrier, 153 154
    pretending to involve others in solving, 149–151
    questions for diagnosing, 146, 155–156
    unfinished business in eliminating, 159–160
Abuse, 56–58
Accountability discussions, 224
    and collaboration, 152
    to discover intentions, 27
    lack of training for, 75–76
    and potentially devastating feedback, 235
    preparation for, 15
    repeated, 22
    self-assessment of skills for, 247–251
    (*See also individual topics*)
Accountability skills, learnability of, 39
Acting out of your concerns, 32–34
Adrenaline, 50, 56, 57, 88, 114, 180, 181
Advice, avoiding, 145–148
Advising, where necessary, 156–159

Agree on a Plan, 195–201, 209
    clear expectations, 199–200
    for difficult problems, 213, 220
    and making assumptions, 197–198
    and predictable bad endings, 196–197
    specific responsibilities, 199
    summarizing conversation, 205 206
    time factors, 200–201
    WWWF, 198–199
Allen, Woody, 1, 189
Allowing violations, 1–6
Ambiguous causes, 140
AMPP model, 185–188
"And" thinking, 37
Anger:
    curiosity vs., 61
    dealing with, 181–190
    dissipating, 182–184
    understanding, 180–181
Asch, Solomon, 35, 62, 229
Asking (AMPP model), 185
Asking for ideas, 148–156
    and avoiding quick advice, 145–148
    and biasing responses, 148–149
    and needing to have all the answers, 151–153
    and pretending to involve others, 149–151
    and sources of influence, 153–156
Asking for permission, 89
Assumptions, 51–53
    revealed through nonverbal communication, 33
    when agreeing on a plan, 197–198
Attribution errors, 52–53 (*See also* Fundamental attribution error)
Attribution studies, 51
Audits, 203

Authoritarian leadership style, 115
Authority, confronting, 226–229

B
Barriers:
  joint exploration of, 145
  motivation, 153, 159–160
  physical, 157–159
  questions for diagnosing, 61, 124,
    146, 155–156
  (*See also* Ability barriers)
Behavior:
  borderline, 237–239
  impacted by data, 68, 158
  impacted by gadgets, 67–68
  natural consequences of, 227
  nonverbal, 33
  stories that justify your worst
    behaviors, 58–59
  unwillingness to behave badly, 7–8
Biasing responses, 148–149
Bierce, Ambrose, 75
Big problems (*see* Difficult problems)
Bookmarks (for staying focused), 166,
  175–177
Borderline behavior, 237–239
Brainstorming:
  to eliminate ability barriers,
    154–156
  in relationship conversations, 233
Breaking from the pack, 229–231
Broken promises, 31
  Contrasting in dealing with, 87
  staying focused on, 170, 178
Bureaucratic barriers, 157–159

C
"Can I . . ." questions, 36
Carlin, George, 47
Carping, 228, 229
Certainty of silence, choosing, 35–38
Challenger space shuttle disaster, 6
Charisma (as motivator), 111–112
Checkback, 205
Checkup, 204–205
Choose *What* and *If*, 18–44, 222–223

about promises clearly broken, 31
about unclear and iffy infractions,
  31–32
case example, 29–30
for difficult problems, 212,
  214–215
getting to the right conversation,
  24–26
and not speaking when you
  should, 32–41
prioritizing issues, 27–28
signs of dealing with wrong
  problem, 19–24
and speaking up when you
  shouldn't, 41–44
Stay Focused and Flexible, 190
unbundling the problem, 26–27
when encountering new problems,
  166–167
Civility, 8–9
Climate for conversations:
  establishing, 47
  in hazardous half minute, 49–50
Commitments:
  broken, 77, 173
  checking for, 206
  and effective solutions, 147
  making it easy to keep (*see* Make
    It Motivating)
Complicated causes, 140–141
Complicated infractions, 9, 77
Complicated problems (*see* Difficult
  problems)
Concerns, acting out of, 32–34
Conclusions:
  harsh, 93–94
  jumping to, 51–53
Create Safety, 73
  Describe the Gap, 102–103
  for difficult problems, 216–217
  Make It Easy, 163
  Make It Motivating, 134
  (*See also individual topics*)
Confronting authority, 226–229
Confucius, 137
Conscience, nagging, 34–35

Consequence bundle, 111
  and perks, 116
  use of power to expand, 113
Consequences:
  explained to resistant workers, 126
  and masked causes, 142
  natural (*see* Natural consequences)
  reasons to explore, 124
  as source of motivation, 134
  and unbundling of problems, 26
Content of infractions, 24, 178
Content–pattern–relationship (CPR)
      model, 24–26
  in analyzing problems, 178–179
  in deciding what to discuss, 28, 45
Contrasting:
  for difficult problems, 216–218
  at end of accountability
      conversation, 200
  when breaking from the
      pack, 230
  when describing the gap, 86–87
  when discussing emergent
      problems, 168, 169
  when discussing repeated
      infractions, 100
Conversing, 228
Coping, 228–229
CPR model (*see* Content–pattern–
      relationship model)
Crimson Tide (film), 112
Critical-event follow-up, 202
Criticism, follow-up perceived as, 203
Crucial accountability, 1–14
  foundation of, 172–174
  learning positive skills for, 12–14
  and positive deviance, 10–12
  providing polite ways for exacting,
      8–9
  with serious/complicated
      infractions, 9
  and unwillingness to behave
      badly, 7–8
  and willingness to allow violations,
      1–6
Crucial Skills newsletter, 246

Culture changes, 236–237
Curiosity, anger vs., 61
Cutting out, 228

D
Data, behavior impacted by, 68, 158
Deadlines, ambiguity in, 201
Delay, strategic, 189, 223
Describe the Gap, 75–103, 223
  for difficult problems, 212,
      217, 218
  end with a question, 97–98
  knowing what not to do, 77–80
  learning from positive deviants
      about, 80–81
  share your path, 91–97
  start with safety, 81–91
  in tough situations, 98–101
Diagnosis of problems, 106
Diagnostic questions, 97–98
Differentiating yourself, 41–43
Difficult problems, 211–224
  Agree on a Plan and Follow Up,
      213, 220
  Choose *What* and *If*, 212,
      214–215
  Make It Safe, 216–218
  Describe the Gap, 212, 217, 218
  Make It Easy, 212, 218–219
  Make It Motivating, 212, 218–219
  Master My Stories, 212, 215–216
  Stay Focused and Flexible,
      213, 219
  (*See also* "Yeah-Buts")
Difficult/unpleasant tasks, 138–143
Dirksen, Everett, 165
Discipline, 127–128
Dishonoring peers, 43–44
Dispositional view:
  and excessive use of power,
      113–114
  situational view vs., 52

E
Effectiveness formula, 147
Ekman, Paul, 33

Emergent problems (*see* Stay Focused and Flexible)
Emotions (feelings):
 dissipating, 182–184
 effect of attempting to hide, 33–34
 explosive (*see* Explosive emotions)
 getting to source of, 184
Empathy (for difficult bosses), 227
Empowerment, involvement and, 148
Ending conversations (*see* Agree on a plan)
Entrapment, 78
Escher, M. C., 258
Exaggerating cost of expressing views, 37–38
Expectations:
 and motivating others, 110–111
 praise for meeting, 256–262
 repeated violations of, 21–22
  (*See also* Violated expectations)
 when agreeing on a plan, 199–200
Explosive emotions, 179–189
 dealing with anger, 181–190
 understanding anger, 180–181

F
Facts:
 for dealing with borderline behavior, 238–239
 when sharing your path, 94–95
Fear:
 and discussions of emergent problems, 168
 as motivator, 115
Feedback:
 asking for, 161
 potentially devastating, 234–235
Feelings (*see* Emotions)
Flexibility (*see* Stay Focused and Flexible)
Focus (*see* Stay Focused and Flexible)
Follow Up, 201–208, 209
 checkup and checkback, 204–205
 for difficult problems, 213, 220
 frequency and type of, 201–205
 and micromanagement or abandonment, 203–204
 problems with, 206–208
 reasons for, 206–208

Force, 114, 115 (*See also* Power)
Forgetting promises, 206–207
Fundamental attribution error, 52, 53
 avoiding, 95
 Contrasting to avoid, 86
 helping others to commit, 55

G
Gadgets, behavior impacted by, 67–68
Games, avoiding, 77–78
Gaps, 76–77 (*See also* Describe the Gap)
Groundhog Day:
 avoiding, 98–101
 eliminating, 24
 and nagging, 242
 and repeated infractions, 22, 25
Groundhog Day (film), 22
Group attacks, 90
Group learning tools, 263

H
Hands-off management style, 204
Hazardous half minute, 49–51
Hearsay, 233–234
Helplessness, 38–39
Hidden victims, 120–121
Human resources:
 and problem employees, 233
 and way out of line people, 236
Humanizing questions, 59
Humor, inappropriate, 90

I
Ideas, asking for (*see* Asking for ideas)
Identifying problems (*see* Choose What and If)
If question (*see* Choose What and If)
Inability to change, 244–246
Influence:
 and commitment-keeping, 153–156
 identifying sources of, 60–68
 personal factors in, 60–61
 social factors in, 61–64
 structural factors in, 64–68
 using sources of, 69–70
Information access, 158

Infractions:
  content of, 24, 178
  pattern of, 24–25, 178
  repeated, 21–26, 100, 241–242
  serious/complicated, 9, 77
  unclear and iffy, 31–32
Innuendo, 78
Intentions, unbundling of problems
    and, 26–27
Involvement:
  to enable others, 146–147
  to motivate others, 147–148
  pretending to involve others,
    149–151

J
Jumping to conclusions, 51–53

L
Lack of motivation, signs of, 106–107
LaMotta, John, 33
Leadership:
  knowledge and, 151
  lack of training for, 76
Leadership styles, 115
Lewin, Kurt, 115
Long-term benefits, 120

M
Make It Easy, 137–163
  by advising where necessary,
    156–159
  by asking for ideas, 148–156
  by avoiding quick advice, 145–148
  and biasing responses, 148–149
  by checking both sides, 159–160
  and confusing motivation and
    ability, 139–143
  for difficult problems, 212, 218–219
  by jointly exploring barriers, 145
  and link between motivation and
    ability, 138–139
  by making it safe, 160–162
  and misdiagnosis of problems,
    138–143
  and needing to have all the
    answers, 151–153
  and pretending to involve others,
    149–151

  skill needed to, 143–145
  and sources of influence, 153–156
Make It Motivating, 105–135, 224
  approaches to avoid, 111–116
  case example, 131–133
  and charisma, 111–112
  and consequence bundle, 111
  and creating work-arounds,
    129–130
  and diagnosis of problems, 106
  for difficult problems, 212,
    218–219
  and expectations, 110–111
  by exploring natural consequences,
    117–123
  finishing conversations about,
    130–131
  by matching methods to
    circumstances, 123–127
  oversimplification in, 107–110
  and perks, 115–116
  and power, 112–115
  signs of lack of motivation,
    106–107
  and use of discipline, 127–128
Manipulation, avoiding, 149–151
Marginal work, 237–239
Marston, Ralph, 211
Masked causes, 141–143
Master My Stories, 47–72, 223
  choosing silence, 53–54
  choosing violence, 54–58
  for difficult problems, 212,
    215–216
  and the hazardous half minute,
    48–51
  in hearsay situations, 234
  with "humanizing questions," 59
  identifying sources of influence in,
    60–68
  jumping to conclusions/making
    assumptions, 51–53
  personal factors in, 60–61
  social factors in, 61–64
  structural factors in, 64–68
  that justify your worst behaviors,
    58–59
  using sources of influence in,
    69–70

Micromanagement, 203–204
Milgram, Stanley, 35, 62
Mirroring (AMPP model), 186
Misdiagnosis of problems, 138–143
Money (as motivator), 65–66
Motivation, 223–224
    ability vs., 153
    confusing ability and, 139–143
    of difficult bosses, 227
    involvement and, 147–148
    lack of, 106–107
    link between ability and,
        138–139
    Master My Stories, 71
    power of any source of, 153
Motivation barriers, ability barriers
    and, 153, 159–160
Move to Action, 193
    Agree on a Plan, 195–201,
        205–206
    Follow Up, 201–208
    (*See also individual topics*)
Mutual Purpose:
    and collaboration, 152
    for difficult problems, 216–217
    when dealing with difficult
        bosses, 227
    when describing the gap, 84,
        87–89
    when discussing overwork
        situations, 240–241
    when discussing repeated
        infractions, 100
Mutual Respect:
    effect of force on, 114
    when describing the gap, 83–85

N
Nagging, 241–242
Nagging conscience, 34–35
Natural consequences:
    in case example, 131–133
    of difficult bosses' behavior, 227
    explaining, to resistant
        workers, 126
    exploring, 117–123
    and masked causes, 142
    as source of motivation, 134

"Nice" (organizational culture),
    207–208
Nietzche, Friedrich, 57
Nonverbal behavior, 33
Not speaking when you should, 32–41
    and acting out of concerns, 32–34
    and choosing certainty of silence,
        35–38
    and feelings of helplessness, 38–39
    and nagging conscience, 34–35

O
On-the-spot creativity (*see* Stay
        Focused and Flexible)
Osgood, Charles, 225
Oversimplification (of motivation),
    107–110
Overwork, 239–241

P
Paddleford, Clementine, 195
Paperwork (as barrier), 158
Paraphrasing (AMPP model),
    186–187
Passing the buck, 78–79
Path to Action:
    in hazardous half minute, 50–51
    of the other person, 184–188
    paraphrasing of, 187–188
    and sources of feelings, 180
    when dealing with explosive
        emotions, 180–181
    when describing the gap, 93
Pattern of infraction, 24–25, 178
Peer pressure, 35, 62–63
Peers, dishonoring, 43–44
Perks (as motivator), 115–116
Permission, asking for, 89
Personal ability barriers, 154–155
Personal factors, in mastering your
        stories, 60–61
Petersen, Donald, 259
Physical barriers, 157–159
Positive deviance, 10–12, 224
Positive deviants, learning from,
        80–81
Potentially devastating feedback,
        234–235

Power:
coping with failure of, 129–130
motivation through, 112–115
Praise, 256–262
for following process, 261
for groups, 261
for individuals, 261
more than you think you should, 257–259
and problem solving, 256–257
spontaneous and structured, 261–262
Predictable bad endings, 196–197
Preparation for Accountability conversations, 15
Priming:
to create safety, 187–188
in relationship conversations, 232–233
when leading root-cause discussions, 161–162
Priorities, differing, 124–125
Prioritizing issues, 27–28
Privacy (for accountability discussions), 89–90
Problem-based relationships, 242–244
Problems:
choosing right problem to address, 223
diagnosis of, 106
with Follow Up, 206–208
misdiagnosis of, 138–143
new problems arise during conversation, 174–179
(*See also* Difficult problems)
Promises:
broken (*see* Broken promises)
forgetting, 206–207
Purpose (*see* Mutual Purpose)

Q
Questions, 223
to ask employees, 151–153
"can I . . .", 36
for diagnosing barriers, 61, 124, 146, 155–156
for diagnosing not speaking up when we should, 32

at end of accountability conversation, 97–98, 100, 200
humanizing, 59
for Six-Source Model, 253–256
when describing the gap, 97–98

R
Reading groups, discussion questions for, 263–264
Recurring/repeating problems, ability barriers and, 155–156
Relationships:
effect of force on, 114
effect of infractions on, 25–26
when dealing with emergent problems, 178–179
Repeated infractions, 21–26
discussing the right issues with, 23–24
Contrasting when discussing, 100
getting increasingly upset about, 22–23
and nagging, 241–242
tools for handling, 24–26
(*See also* Groundhog Day)
Resistance:
effect of force on, 115
overcoming, 125–127
Respect:
Mutual, 83–85, 114
when describing the gap, 83–87
Responsibilities, specific, 199
Rewards (as motivator), 65, 115–116
Right conversation, getting to the, 24–26
Risk:
of project for which follow-up is needed, 202
of speaking up, 35–38
Root causes:
asking for permission to discuss, 160–161
identifying, 156
priming to ease discussion of, 161–162
Six-Source Model, 60
Rules (as barriers), 157–158

S

Safety:
    and asking for permission, 89
    creating, 73
    effect of force on, 115
    to make commitment-keeping
        easy, 160–162
    mutual purpose for, 84, 87–89
    mutual respect for, 83–87
    privacy for, 89–90
    signs that safety is at risk, 82–83
    in starting conversations, 81–91
    watching for safety problems,
        96–97
    when breaking from the pack,
        230–231
    when dealing with anger, 181–182,
        187–189
    when dealing with difficult
        bosses, 227
    when people feel unsafe, 168–169
Sandwiching, 77
Scary people, 235–236
Scheduled follow-up, 202
Self-assessment of skills, 247–251
Serious infractions, 9, 77
Sharing your path, 91–97
    avoiding judgments/harsh
        conclusions in, 93–94
    and keeping others in the dark,
        92–93
    and sharing your story, 95–97
    start with facts in, 94–95
Short-term benefits, 119
"Should I . . ." questions, 36
Silence:
    choosing, 53–54
    choosing certainty of, 35–38
    and difficult problems, 222
    in face of violated expectations,
        2–8
    warning signs of going to, 39–41
Situational view, 52, 59
Six-Source Model:
    diagnostic questions, 252–255
    for difficult problems, 218–219
    Make It Easy, 153–154, 212

    Make It Motivating, 116, 212
    Master My Stories, 68–71
    structure of, 60–68
Skills self-assessment, 247–251
Social ability barriers, 155
Social factors, in mastering your
        stories, 61–64
Social norms, violations of, 1–4
Solutions, commitment and, 147
Speaking up when you shouldn't,
        41–44
    and differentiating yourself from
        others, 41–43
    and dishonoring peers, 43–44
Standards:
    clarifying, 236
    holding people to, 42–44
Stay Focused and Flexible, 165–191
    for difficult problems, 213, 219
    need for, 166–167
    when explosive emotions take over,
        179–189
    when new problems arise, 174–179
    when people feel unsafe, 168–169
    when your trust has been violated,
        169–174
Stepping out of content, 97, 101,
        132, 133
Stepping out of the conversation,
        122, 168
Sticky problems (*see* Difficult
        problems)
Stories, mastering (*see* Master
        My Stories)
Strategic delay, 189, 223
Structural factors:
    and ability barriers, 155
    in mastering your stories, 64–68
Summarizing (planning discussion),
        205–206
Surprise attacks, 78

T

Tactically inferior solutions, 147
Threats, consequences as, 121–122
Time factors, in agreeing on a plan,
        200–201

Topics of conversations (*see* Choose *What* and *If*)
Trust:
    creating bedrock of, 174
    violation of, 169–174

U
Unbundling problems, 26–27
Unclear infractions, 31–32
Uncommunicative spouses, 231–233
Unexpected events (*see* Stay Focused and Flexible)

V
Victims, hidden, 120–121
Violated expectations:
    dangerous situations created by, 229
    defined, 76
    as gaps, 76–77
    providing polite ways for dealing with, 8–9
    repeated instances of, 21–22
    willingness to allow, 1–6
    (*See also* Broken promises)
Violated trust, 169–174
Violence, 54–58
    physical, 181–182
    verbal, 7, 222

W
Washington, Denzel, 112
Way out of line people, 235–236
What conversations to have (*see* Choose *What* and *If*)

What not to do, 77–80
Whether to have conversations (*see* Choose *What* and *If*)
Work on Me First, 15
    Choose *What* and *If*, 45
    (*See also individual topics*)
Work-arounds, creating, 129–130
Workload, 239–241
Worry, 207–208
Wrong problem, signs of dealing with, 19–24
WWWF model, 198–199

Y
"Yeah-Buts," 225–246
    borderline behavior, 237–239
    breaking from the pack, 229–231
    confronting authority, 226–229
    culture changes, 236–237
    hearsay, 233–234
    inability to change, 244–246
    nagging, 241–242
    overwork, 239–241
    potentially devastating feedback, 234–235
    problem-based relationships, 242–244
    uncommunicative spouses, 231–233
    way out of line or scary people, 235–236

Z
Zone of acceptance, 31, 40, 242

About the Authors

This award-winning team of authors has produced four *New York Times* best-sellers—*Crucial Conversations: Tools for Talking when Stakes are High* (2002), *Crucial Accountability: Tools for Resolving Violated Expectations, Broken Commitments, and Bad Behavior* (2005), *Influencer: The New Science of Leading Change* (2008), and *Change Anything: The New Science of Personal Success* (2011). They are also cofounders of VitalSmarts, an innovator in corporate training and organizational performance.

Kerry Patterson has authored award-winning training programs and led multiple long-term change efforts. In 2004, he received the BYU Marriott School of Management Dyer Award for outstanding contribution in organizational behavior. He completed doctoral work at Stanford University.

Joseph Grenny is an acclaimed keynote speaker and consultant who has implemented major corporate change initiatives for the past thirty years. He is also a cofounder of Unitus Labs, a not-for-profit organization that helps the world's poor achieve economic self-reliance.

David Maxfield is a leading researcher, consultant, and speaker. He has led research studies on the role of human behavior in medical errors, safety hazards, and project execution. He completed doctoral work in psychology at Stanford University.

Ron McMillan is a sought-after speaker and consultant. He cofounded the Covey Leadership Center, where he served as vice president of research and development. He has worked with leaders ranging from first-level managers to executives from the Fortune 500.

Al Switzler is a renowned consultant and speaker who has directed training and management initiatives with leaders from dozens of Fortune 500 companies worldwide. He also served on the faculty of the Executive Development Center at the University of Michigan.

About **Vital**Smarts

An innovator in corporate training and leadership development, VitalSmarts combines three decades of original research with 50 years of the best social science thinking to help organizations achieve new levels of performance. Specifically, we focus on human behavior—the underlying written and unwritten rules that shape what employees do every day and create the cultural operating system upon which an organization functions.

VitalSmarts' work within the halls of some of the world's top organizations has led us to identify four skill sets present in successful companies. When used in combination, these high-leverage skills create healthy corporate cultures that spur flawless execution and consistent innovation. These skill sets are taught in our award-winning training programs and *New York Times* bestselling books of the same titles: *Crucial Conversations*, *Crucial Accountability*, *Influencer*, and *Change Anything*.

VitalSmarts has trained more than one million people worldwide and helped more than 300 of the Fortune 500 realize significant results using this proven method for driving rapid, sustainable and measurable change in behaviors. VitalSmarts has been ranked by *Inc.* magazine as one of the fastest-growing companies in America for eight consecutive years.

www.vitalsmarts.com

SPECIAL VALUE FOR BOOK READERS

Authors Joseph Grenny, Kerry Patterson, Al Switzler, David Maxfield, and Ron McMillan are offering book readers the following **FREE resources (a $275 value).** All you have to do is go online to get them. Read on.

Access the VitalSmarts Video Vault

Not sure how to approach an accountability conversation you know you should be holding?

Take your accountability discussions to the next level by watching videos of skills taught in the book.

Authors' Discussion Questions

Use these relevant discussion questions to guide your next book club or reading group. You'll strengthen your skills by learning with others.

Listen to Audio Lessons from the Authors

Get access to exclusive bonus material from the authors in our popular Crucial Accountability Audio Companion, and hear them share entertaining stories and insights.

Join the *Crucial Skills Newsletter* Community

Did you find Ch. 9, "The 12 'Yeah-Buts,'" helpful? Subscribe to our weekly e-newsletter and ask your own tough "yeah, but." The authors answer a reader's question each week, providing powerful insights into the tough, real-world issues you face.

To access these resources, visit **www.vitalsmarts.com/bookresources**.